Advance Praise for *She's My Dad*

"*She's My Dad* is the missing link in the LGBTQ+ narrative. When Williams discovers that his father is transgender, he is forced to confront his own identity and, consequently, reevaluate everything he's ever known to be true. Written with gut-wrenching honesty and a raw vulnerability that exposes both deep pain and deep compassion, this gripping memoir of love and loss reveals the heartache and the beauty of navigating life when a family member comes out. A much-welcomed addition to the library of LGBTQ+ resources and one I highly recommend!"
—Amber Cantorna, National Speaker, Leader, and
Author of *Refocusing My Family* and *Unashamed: A
Coming-Out Guide for LGBTQ Christians*

"In *She's My Dad*, Jonathan Williams manages to honestly capture the pain and heartbreak he felt during his parent's transition without discounting the reality of Paula's identity. As someone who has dealt with family rejection, I kept tensing up as I read, waiting for the moment when the suffering of these two people would be pitted against each other—when we'd be forced to see one of them as the bad guy. Instead, Jonathan and Paula work together to show us a reality in which two people in difficult circumstances can journey through pain and toward a new relationship, thanks to a heavy helping of grace."
—Austen Hartke, Author of *Transforming: The Bible
and the Lives of Transgender Christians*

"When a parent begins living their gender identity authentically, it impacts the identity of everyone in the family. In *She's My Dad*, Jonathan Williams describes the pain of reconceiving his father and himself, both as individuals and as pastors. Williams's honest portrayal illustrates how crises can ultimately lead to an expansion of our understanding of God—reflecting the truth of Paula Stone Williams's belief that the quest for authenticity is holy, sacred, and for the greater good. The book is a wonderful resource for transitioning people, their love and those who are exploring how God is working in our era to us from the trap of tribal theologies."
—Suzanne DeWitt Hall, Author of *Transfigured: A 40-Day j
through Scripture for Gender-Queer and Transgender*

"In a raw and authentic voice, Jonathan Williams has given us mate look at his journey through his father's transition. This is often overlooked, and one we need to hear. He takes us all t through his vulnerable and painful coming-to-terms and out th

side into the light of a Christianity of radical love and inclusion—the vision Jesus had in mind all along! For anyone seeking to understand the broader picture of a family in transition, this is well worth the read."
—Susan Cottrell, Founder, FreedHearts.org, and Author of *"Mom, I'm Gay": Loving Your LGBTQ Child and Strengthening Your Faith*

"True human connection happens on the other side of life's deepest pain. Jonathan Williams gives us an unfiltered window in to his journey of watching his father transition to a woman, providing us the hard-earned gift of witnessing true human connection emerge. In this raw and tear-stained memoir, we follow Jonathan as he discovers the most unexpected invitation to live in the way of Jesus, and in choosing the narrow, difficult, painful path, he shows us all the way to a life worth living."
—Colby Martin, Teaching Pastor, Sojourn Grace Collective, and Author of *UnClobber: Rethinking Our Misuse of the Bible on Homosexuality*

"Williams confronts the mystery and struggle of what it means to live a life of truth and authenticity for himself and for his father. He criss-crosses pronouns and names, shows us that naming is our way out of isolation, and draws on his experience as a son, father, husband, and pastor in telling his story. He reminds us that we belong to each other, that by working through the pain that sometimes comes with acceptance, we're given new ties that we never thought possible. This book is important reading for anyone who has confronted change in their families or a crisis of faith. He also gives words to the complex experience of having a parent who is transgender. He articulates how it's possible to both miss someone as they were and celebrate who they are today. This book is a gift."
—Heather Bryant, Writer and COLAGE Ambassador

"Jonathan and Paula Williams have given us an incredibly valuable gift. In a time when so many are debating about trans identities, people's stories bring to life what is truly important—how to love one another when someone in the family comes out. As the son of a parent who comes out as trans, Jonathan Williams helps us to see the deep struggle of grief and denial, and ultimately acceptance. Meanwhile, Paula shows us what a deeply parental love looks like in trying to care for one's family while living her own life truthfully, even if it means losing one's tribe. Through deeply honest storytelling, Jonathan and Paula Williams have been able to nuance and humanize the conversation in a way that theology books never could. Their story is one that needs to be heard, especially in the evangelical world of this generation."
—Pastor Danny Cortez, Founder, Estuary Space (estuaryspace.org)

SHE'S MY DAD

A Father's Transition and a Son's Redemption

JONATHAN WILLIAMS
WITH PAULA STONE WILLIAMS

WESTMINSTER
JOHN KNOX PRESS
LOUISVILLE · KENTUCKY

© 2019 Jonathan Williams

First edition
Published by Westminster John Knox Press
Louisville, Kentucky

19 20 21 22 23 24 25 26 27 28—10 9 8 7 6 5 4 3 2 1

Unless otherwise indicated, Scripture quotations are from the New Revised Standard Version of the Bible, copyright © 1989 by the Division of Christian Education of the National Council of the Churches of Christ in the U.S.A., and are used by permission.

Book design by Drew Stevens
Cover art and design by Stephen Brayda

Library of Congress Cataloging-in-Publication Data is on file at the
Library of Congress, Washington, D.C.

ISBN: 978-0-664-26435-2

Most Westminster John Knox Press books are available at special quantity discounts when purchased in bulk by corporations, organizations, and special-interest groups. For more information, please e-mail SpecialSales@wjkbooks.com.

*To my wife, Jubi, who walked alongside me
each step of my journey with amazing grace
and unending love. Thank you.*

CONTENTS

ACKNOWLEDGMENTS

I'm thankful to so many who helped me to tell such an important story. To Westminster John Knox Press, thank you for taking a chance on our story. Jessica Miller Kelley, thanks for walking with me throughout the writing and publishing process. I'm especially grateful for the challenge of creating greater clarity in my own story. You've made me a better writer and storyteller. To Sarah Ngu, who thought this story was important enough to let the world know, and to John Leland who beautifully told the first iteration of this story for the *New York Times*, I give many thanks.

I'm grateful for friends along the way who've heard this story manifested in all manners and forms and continue to be a huge support. To our Carroll Gardens Crew, the Crosses, Scazzariellos, Sterns, George Fuchs, Ihrigs, and Jason Sanders: thanks for listening during the late nights and self-doubts. A special thanks to Nicole, Anu, and Lila, who aren't just great friends but incredibly hospitable: thanks for gifting me with a safe place to write. Thanks to my Long Island Guys, Adam, Chris, CK, Bobby, Shango, Autz, and Greg, who know my story at its best . . . and worst. I'm thankful to the Holy Smokes and our holier conversations. I'm thankful to Stef Fontela, who created space for our family to tell this story and in the process became family herself.

Forefront Church in Brooklyn has changed my life. To Ben, Jen, Bobby, and Mira: you lived this with me, and I'm better for having you a part of it. Thanks to each of you in this church who give me far more than I could ever give you. Thank you for allowing me the time and space to share this with you all.

I'm thankful for my spiritual family outside of New York, the W/ group, Jared, Steph, Ryjo, Young, and Michelle. Life with each of you brings me energy and joy. You've dissected, processed, and listened. I owe you.

Thanks to my own family, the Mathew Seven, Biju and Ana, and especially my in-laws, Saramma and C.C. Abraham. Each of you is quick to love, filled with grace, and always shows me Christ. To Gramma Faust, who gave me great insight on your calling and mission; it wasn't easy but I'm grateful for it.

Jana, Jael, and Kijana, my God, I doubt I'm alive without each of you. Each step of the way with you has been painful, hard, and absolutely beautiful. Thanks for telling your story and letting me share your insights. Mom, your quiet strength never ceases to amaze. Your encouragement in the midst of pain continues to inspire. Thank you is not enough.

Dad, it's never easy, but you've been only gracious. Thank you for your wisdom and compassion, which let me find myself in your story. You let me bare my soul and, in the process, yours too. With that soul-baring came opportunities for anger and frustration. Instead, I received only encouragement to move forward on this journey. Thank you for that gracious love. It means the world. You've let me heal, sometimes at your expense, and for that I'll always be grateful.

My Asha and Lyla, I love you both infinitely. I don't know if it's possible to love either of you more. And finally, to my wife, Jubi, who lived out my dad's transition with me. You literally switched professions, did more than your fair share of parenting, and gave me literal space so I could write. When I came back from writing emotionally exhausted, you gave me peace and security. There is no amount of thanks for you. To say that the past few years have been tough is an understatement, and yet I'll look back on them fondly because I got to live them with you. I love you.

Chapter 1

THE VISIT

There was a moment I thought my father might be a woman. The thought came in the midst of a hockey fight between two now forgotten players from the New York Islanders and the Philadelphia Flyers at the old Nassau Coliseum.

I myself hoped to become a man. At thirteen years old, my prepubescent body didn't bear any of the physical markings of manhood. I prayed to be even five feet tall and weigh at least one hundred pounds. I prayed for some physical evidence that I was coming into my manhood. My body already betrayed me as my physical growth—and with it my masculine confidence—lagged behind the behemoths in my junior high school. For the time being, I prayed a great prayer that I'd soon grow into a man, and in the meantime, remained embarrassed that despite my "teen" age, I was still a child.

The hockey fight gave me a chance to express my hope in stereotypical manhood. As the players brawled, I brought forth every bit of my innate masculinity and cursed. It was my duty. The guttural response was overcompensation for what my body had not yet become. "F*ck yeah!" I cheered and pounded the Plexiglas. My scream was an assertion that, while there may not be any physical evidence, I was nonetheless a man. I was as much of a man as the blue-collar hockey fans who screamed and cursed around me; these men with their calloused hands, beards, and t-shirts too tight from years of their bodies being of secondary importance to the hustle of their economic livelihood. I was as much of a man as the businessmen at the game who screamed with me in their loosened ties, top button undone, and beer in hand. Their yelling was as much a response to their daily commute to solve the world's financial problems a few short miles away in New York City. Here they were free to be their primal selves. And so I screamed in approval at the punches being thrown between the two players who lived out the epitome of their manhood and asserted my right to join them in mine.

My father was in every sense a man. He stood at well over six feet, weighed a healthy sum, and had full, black chest hair that I prayed would soon come to exist on me. I didn't measure up to my father, but knew it was only a matter of time before I had the same physical stature, the same chest hair, and maybe even a beard. One could dream! It was only a matter of time before I became a physically imposing presence like my father. It was only a matter of time before I could bring about a level of quiet intimidation, demand excellence of everyone—from family to the cashier at our local deli. It was only a matter of time until heavy footsteps on the hardwood floors of our split-level home would announce my presence too. It was only a matter of time before my own children would run up the stairs at the sound of those footsteps in equal parts awe and adoration. It would be only a matter of time before I too would become a man, just like my father.

For now, I cursed at a hockey game. My father did not. My father sat upright in his seat, legs crossed, clapping politely at the fight just feet away. He wore khakis, a button-down shirt, and loafers to the game, not because he was solving the world's financial problems with the loosened-tie guys, but because it was his outfit of choice. He didn't fit with the blue-collar workers either. He was somewhere else. While one might assume that my father's traditionally feminine body language accounted for me questioning his gender, it was not. Nor was it the consciously conservative attire that made him stand out that particular evening.

The fleeting moment that I thought my father could be a woman came in response to his smile.

I often smile when I'm confused. I smile when I have no earthly idea about the medical procedure I'm discussing with my doctor. I smile when I can't grasp the depth of my friend's great theological discovery. Someone's musings across a crowded bar will go unheard, and I will smile. I'll often smile when I'm confused by the words or actions of a stranger. When I'm intimidated, I smile. My default in any uncomfortable and confusing circumstance is to grin with sureness. While my brain might not comprehend a single thing, my facial expression shows a knowing confidence. I learned that from my father.

My father smiled and it belied his enjoyment of the fight before us. My father's smile feigned camaraderie with the other fans but exposed a deep discord. The enjoyment of watching a hockey fight is not a prerequisite of any partic-ular gender, but at this moment my father's smile revealed the painful truth that there was no common connection to the innate longings of his thirteen-year-old son. My father sat with his legs crossed, clapping, with a smile on his face, and for a fleeting moment, I thought that my dad might not be a man.

"I think you know why I'm calling," he said.

I received an urgent message from my father telling me that he needed to fly from his home in Denver to come talk to me where my family lived in Brooklyn, New York. I called back right away.

Twenty-three years had passed since my fleeting doubt about my father's manhood, and the hockey game was barely a part of my consciousness. In that time I had changed, but not as I hoped. I looked younger than my thirty-six years, could barely grow a beard, and despite a six-inch growth spurt during my freshman year of high school, I never quite made it to the height of my father. I didn't live up to my expectations. In some ways I still waited for the physical attributes of manhood. I lazily relied on male stereotypes to assert my manhood. I was the aggressor at all perceived injustice. When the kid down the street made a derogatory comment about my sister, it was me who left a bruise on his forehead. When a car stopped and cat-called some of my female friends, I challenged the driver to get out and fight, because that's the stereotype of what strong men do. The man who flippantly commented on my dog backed down when I berated him just inches from his face. I exhibited the banal traits of manhood that my body could not. I married a woman I love dearly, had two children, worked first as a teacher and then as the founding pastor of a brand-new church plant that launched just three months prior to my father's phone call. My social attributes left no doubt. I was a leader, an influencer, a vision-caster, a father, and husband—all things to which men have traditionally been taught to aspire.

My dad was my best friend and mentor. It was safe to say that he was my hero.

When I was four years old, I went on a special trip with my dad to Disney World. My parents were young and had no money, so we stayed at my great-grandmother's trailer right outside of Tampa. We drove to Disney World in a little Mercury Lynx and sang "Dixieland Delight" by Alabama. When a ride on the Tea Cups kept my father up all night with crippling vertigo, he still managed to take me back to Disney's Magic Kingdom the next day. My father sat beside me as we rode Race Cars, literally ad nauseam. I steered the car, and my father, with his foot on the gas, made the car go.

I wanted nothing more than to please my dad. As an eleven-year-old Little League baseball player I went through a bit of a slump. In fact, I didn't get a single hit the entire season. The season before, I had been an All-Star. When my dad went to speak at churches, he told the staff, elders, and every little old lady who walked into church about his All-Star son. After one failed at-bat I started crying. I didn't cry because I was frustrated or felt bad for our team. I cried because I was sure that my father was disappointed.

Each day, my sisters and I ran upstairs to greet our father. Would Dad be in a good mood and ready to talk? Would we find love from our dad? Would he be too frustrated to talk with us? My father could love with abandon in one moment and create fear in another.

My father once spent a year reading *The Chronicles of Narnia* to me. In one famous passage, Lucy Pevensie asks, "'Then [Aslan the Lion] isn't safe?' said Lucy. 'Safe?' said Mr. Beaver; 'don't you hear what Mrs. Beaver tells you? Who said anything about safe? 'Course he isn't safe. But he's good.'"[1] My father was my god. He wasn't safe. But he was really good.

As I got older, we climbed mountains together, my father withholding his strength so that his son could lead the way up the trail. At dinner I drove the conversation toward the deeper questions of life. My father was a pastor, but even my doubts were safe with him. "Is there even a God? . . . I think that the church may have it wrong when it comes to evolution. . . . Is it possible that the Bible is not inerrant?" My father gently responded with more questions and delighted in the fact that his son looked for the gray in the midst of black-and-white. It was that easy rhythm that eventually pushed me toward ministry.

My father directed a church-planting organization in the Northeastern U.S., and while his official role was director, he was a pastor. My father was a church speaker who visited churches across America. At thirty-six years of age my father became the youngest speaker at our denomination's national convention. He regularly spoke to crowds of thousands at some of the biggest churches in America. My father was an editor for our denomination's oldest magazine. His words carried respectable weight in the almost six thousand churches that were a part of our denomination.[2] His best friends were popular speakers, writers, and Evangelical Christian influencers. It wasn't out of the ordinary to hear my father and his friends politicize on the current state of Evangelical affairs, knowing full well that they were the ones with the power to shift the Evangelical landscape. I'd sit on the pink carpet in my father's office, waiting for him to finish a phone call. I listened intently while my father brought gentle encouragement to a pastor going through the struggles of leading a church in one call and then give a stern warning to another pastor over his narrow-mindedness in the next (all the pastors in this church were men). The stature that my father held at home was doubly true in his profession. Other people steered, but my father's foot was on the gas. My father and his personality were larger than life. My father knew that he was my hero. He knew that other young pastors in the denomination called him their hero too.

As an adult, I joined up with the church-planting organization of which my father was chairman of the board. It was my father's job to create new churches, and through those connections I was hired to start a church in Brooklyn. My father made sure that my family was put in a situation to succeed.

I was a pastor like my dad. Now my father was my professional mentor and helper. There were more questions. "Dad, how in the world do you raise money? . . . At what point should we launch our Sunday services? . . . I'm still not sure I believe in God. . . . Am I even qualified to lead this thing?" The rhythm between my father and me intrinsically bound us, with no event too profound and no feeling too small. The rhythm was easy and familiar. Our relationship was sure and steady.

"No, Dad," I replied. "I don't know why you're calling or why the family is flying out here so suddenly."

We'd been on the phone just two days earlier, talking about the success of my new church plant. Things can happen in two days. Was my father dying of cancer? A few years prior, my mother told my father that she was taking a job in Colorado. "You can leave New York and come with me if you'd like. I'm going." My father acquiesced, and my parents moved out west. Perhaps he was leaving my mother. Anxiety welled up, my insides blown and scattered, as my body remained intact. My friend's parents divorced when we were in high school, and he still bears the scars today. We had talked about it over beers.

"It doesn't matter that we're adults," my friend said. "That pain is still fresh." I braced for pain. Was there an arrest? I couldn't see my father as a hardened criminal, but maybe insurance fraud? I'd had my own legal issues and came out just fine. My father must have cheated on my mom, lost his job, or committed a crime. Racing minds did not do my thoughts justice.

"Dad, I have no idea what this is about. Don't make we wait until you come here."

"Please, Jonathan, please just wait until I arrive."

I walked down the block and passed the really good chicken and waffle place my dad and I visited the last time he came to New York. Anxiety riddled my body. I didn't want to eat. I told my wife that my entire family was visiting in two days.

The couch was too short and hard to nap on. The fabric was too hot. We kept the entertainment system because it was only two years old, but it fit awkwardly in our new apartment. Our color scheme was drab. There was too much gray. Maybe some throw pillows would change things? The bookshelf stores only the books that we're not embarrassed to own. I don't have enough skill to mount my flat-screen TV on the wall, even though it would save a ton of space.

A room is just a room. We take it for granted and don't give our space a ton of thought until our space becomes disrupted. Then we assess everything. My father sat in a too-small chair. I made a mental note that we needed to replace it with a loveseat.

My sisters and mom sat on the too-small couch, and my wife brought a chair from the dining room table. We sat in a circle with my father at the head of the room, each of us waiting in solemn anticipation.

"I am transgender," he said.

At least he didn't get arrested. The brief relief I felt shifted quickly. From deep in the recesses of my brain I pulled up all of the connotations about being trans . . . gender? Trans . . . sexual?

My father explained what it meant to have gender identity disorder. My father's words were clinical. Logical.

When my father wants to make something okay he takes away the strength of the words. They no longer carry emotional weight. They sound copied from a professional journal. "Yes, there's going to be an emergency landing in this extreme weather, and yes, the plane might crash. But see, pilots have on-board forward-looking radar wind-shear detectors, which should stop us from dying." And suddenly a near-death experience is nothing more than a premature landing.

My father's explanation of gender identity disorder means nothing. The words have lost their emotion, and I don't even know what he means. That stupid chair is not only too small but it's stained, changed from a gleaming white to a dirty gray, and I need to get rid of it now. My sister says something about how it's great that everyone is okay and it's not cancer or anything life threatening. She tells us that we're all still alive. Except my dad is not alive. He clicks through the *DSM-4* and *-5*,[3] talking about the possible ways the synapses and receptors in his brain might have come to the conclusion that he's really a woman. He's academic in his descriptions and uncomfortable in his skin, and he wants to move along, possibly to the good chicken and waffle place. This is all okay because I'm still here and alive. He smiles.

I don't know how to reply.

"Dad, for a couple of years I've noticed that your ego is oversized. . . . Dad, I notice that you have less influence in Christian circles lately. Is this a way to reclaim influence? . . . Are you trying to garner attention? Look at the way we're all sitting right now. . . . You draw attention to yourself, reference your popular friends, and make sure that everyone knows that you've received the big awards and accolades. . . . What are you trying to prove, Dad?"

And now my father is beaten, and I'm worried because I've never seen him look like this before.

"If it's not your ego, are you dealing with mental illness? It runs in our family. You've been depressed before. There was the time that you left our vacation early because you couldn't get up to go out with us. You were depressed. Your anxiety is legendary, and each one of us in this room shares those traits too. We've been stuck before. . . . Are you sure that you're not sick right now? Are the chemicals in your brain reacting appropriately, and do you need help? Dad this is some ploy to . . ." And my voice trailed off.

My mom and sisters sat silently. My father had already told them the news; they'd had their chance to ask the questions, grasp at straws, and speak in hastened and honest tones with little forethought. My wife walked to the kitchen.

My words bring with them immediate guilt. It's possible that I am blaming him for my worst traits. It's possible that I'm simply projecting my own shortcomings on my father's reason for being transgender. My father has an ego, but so do I. Like my dad, I care about what people think. I want to be the center of attention. I struggle with the same depression and anxiety. But I don't want to be a woman.

My youngest sister reacted differently, thinking at first that it meant our dad likes both men and women.

"I started staring at his shoes thinking they looked feminine," she told me, "and then I hugged him and felt confused, like it was a dream. My dad was hurting, and I knew, no matter what, I accepted him; but it was so sad to see his pain and him so vulnerable. Excruciating."

During that hug, Dad clarified that it meant that he was a woman, and my sister was shocked, feeling as if he had just confessed to murdering someone.

"Then, he and Mom spent the next four hours explaining, and I felt bad for him and for her. But in the back of my head I felt betrayed. It felt like a dream. They shared a video, and I couldn't believe they would share a video to help explain. The guy in the video wasn't like my dad at all! How can I be expected to compare this guy/girl to my dad!

"Every time he left the room that day, I was so scared he would come back dressed as a woman! I was sure he would. And the image I had in my mind was awful. When we got into the car, [our middle sister] said she couldn't tell our husbands. So I called them, and in a matter-of-fact tone said, 'Our dad is a woman; please order Chinese food and get wine.' When we got back to my house, we ate, got drunk, and cried."

My middle sister was more objective. "No one's dying, and our dad has to live out his truth. Maybe things will never be the same, but I can't be the reason that my dad can't live out his truth." She's the most levelheaded. I can't identify.

I told my friend Chris, and he immediately asked the bartender for Jameson. My father had performed his wedding just two years earlier. His denial was strong. "I don't believe you," he said. "In fact, you're full of sh*t. Here's a shot."

—

I Googled: "how to respond when your father says he's transgender." There are transgender support groups for parents who have transitioning kids but nothing for kids with transitioning parents. "New York has 8.5 million people, and none of these motherf*ckers have parents who have transitioned?" Denial is the first step, but it was anger on the tip of my tongue. I didn't want to start a support group. I wanted someone to tell me how to react.

There's no handbook. There's no "how to" on You-Tube. We're rightly creating a culture where those who identify as being transgender receive greater support, but behind every coming-out party, there is a family that's weeping, drinking too much, and Googling what exactly it means to be transgender.

So what does it mean? Is it the same as being *transsexual*? That word carries some negative stigmas. Was my dad transsexual? While I'm at it, what's the difference between someone who is transgender and someone who cross-dresses, sometimes called a *transvestite*? My father is transgender. Does that mean he's now gay and attracted to men? The questions were dizzying. My father came out right before mainstream media highlighted the issues. There was no *Orange Is the New Black*, Caitlin Jenner, or *Transparent* to help normalize the confusion of my dad's announcement. Trying to find answers was even more difficult.

Being transgender means that one's gender, identity, expression, or role does not match up with the sex the person was assigned at birth.[4]

According to Dr. Walter Bockting, a leading expert on gender identity at Columbia University, just because one identifies as transgender does not mean that the person will transition to living out the preferred gender role.[5] Some who identify as transgender will wear the clothing of the preferred identity only in certain social situations. Others will take on the qualities, mannerisms, and norms of the preferred identity but will not dress differently, take hormones, or make bodily changes to better reflect the preferred gender identity.[6]

Even at a young age, my father knew that his gender identity and expression did not match up with the male sex he was assigned at birth. From the age of four, my father knew that he was transgender.

But was my father transsexual? Those who decide to make changes to their bodies through hormone therapies or gender confirmation surgeries are traditionally called *transsexual*. While this term is no longer popular, and its acceptability varies from person to person, it has no connotation around the act of intercourse, fetishes, or anything like the "depraved acts" that the word initially conjured up in my mind. This was a relief, and yet I still struggled with the word. Others in the trans community still work to shed the word *transsexual*. Those who have surgeries or take hormones simply call themselves "trans" or categorize themselves under the banner of being transgender.

As I tried to understand what this news meant for my father and my family, I traveled deeper down the rabbit hole that is sexuality and gender. One of the biggest misconceptions—and one that I certainly believed—was that if one was transgender it also meant that their sexual orientation changed with their bodies. When my father told us he would begin living life full-time as a woman, I very quickly wanted to know if that meant he was sexually attracted to men.

In actuality, sexual orientation is different from gender identity. One's sexual orientation "describes the relationship between who we are (our own gender identity) and who we are attracted to (others' gender identities)."[7] When I asked my dad if he was now gay, the answer was, technically, yes. The gender my father was attracted to didn't change, but his gender did. My father was still very much attracted to women, making him a lesbian. This fact brought about a bit of humor in an otherwise confusing and often exhausting trek through the various categories, terms, and identities of gender and sexuality, all of which remain fluid, depending on the person with whom we're conversing.

Shortly after my father's coming out, I received a message from a pastor with whom I last spoke years ago. This pastor was very curious as to whether or not my father was a transvestite—yet another "trans" word to explore. My familiarity with the word *transvestite* came from the cult classic movie *Rocky Horror Picture Show*. Was it possible that my father was just a classier version of a young, cross-dressing Tim Curry? After a quick look in the dictionary, I replied to this pastor with the meaning of the word *transvestite*:

> A person who wears clothes designed for the opposite sex: a cross-dresser
>
> An older term for crossdresser is *transvestite*. Crossdressers often dress only in certain situations. They do not usually identify as transgender—most identify as straight men.[8]

I informed my pastor acquaintance that, by definition, it was highly unlikely my father was a transvestite as he did identify as transgender. I gently asked my pastor acquaintance if it was possible that *he* was a transvestite. I have yet to receive a response.

Learning about the literally hundreds of combinations of gender identity, biological sex, and sexual orientation, I finally had a better idea of who my dad was. My dad would now identify as a woman. My dad would have surgeries and take hormones to change her biology to reflect a more traditionally female appearance. My father's forthcoming transition was not sexual in any way. It was not a fetish, and it was not depraved, as my limited knowledge previously allowed me to believe. My father was transgender, and was transitioning to live out an expression of who he truly felt he was.

But learning these terms and definitions intellectually did not change the emotional impact of who my father was and was becoming. I still struggled to understand the root cause that brought about such utter destruction and grief to my life. It began to dawn on me that the simple and easy rhythm in which we shared our lives would forever be different. I couldn't conceptualize this difference. When one goes through the trauma of a parent changing gender, the default is to maintain one's framework for looking at the world; I attempted to do so. Up until this point, my limited worldview knew gender only as binary. Gender was biologically assigned based on genitalia, and I had no need to know or learn otherwise. With my father's announcement, however, I quickly realized that my continued limited knowledge of gender would be impossible.

Without a framework, it was easy for me to be angry with my father and his need for attention. It was easy for me to decide that his transition was caused by all of his worst traits. It was convenient for me to believe that this could be fixed. This was all a lie, and, with therapy, my father could return to "normal."

The maddening aspect of gender identity disorder is that the medical community still has very little knowledge of what causes it. Many of the psychological studies surrounding gender identity have been largely discredited, and most who work in the field of gender identity will concede that they've seen only the tip of the iceberg when it comes to genetic causes for gender identity that is inconsistent with physical sex. Of the numerous studies published in the recent past, there are two consistent findings that stand out and bring credence to the idea that gender identity is indeed genetic. A paper written by Katherine J. Wu at Harvard University highlights these findings:

> In 1995 and 2000, two independent teams of researchers decided to examine a region of the brain called the bed nucleus of the stria terminalis (BSTc) in trans- and cisgender men and women. The BSTc functions in anxiety, but is, on average, twice as large and twice as densely populated with cells in men compared to women. This sexual dimorphism is pretty robust, and though scientists don't know why it exists, it appears to be a good marker of a "male" vs. "female" brain.[9]

In simpler terms, researchers have come to a consensus that our brains are *dimorphic*. That means there is a difference between males and females that goes beyond the reproductive body parts with which we're born. These differences can be found in the white matter of our brains.

The U.S. National Library of Medicine study also confirms that gender goes beyond our reproductive organs. In the brains of people assigned male at birth who identified as transgender females, they found that the white matter of their brains closely resembled female white matter rather than the white matter of their assigned sex at birth. The same can be said of those designated female at birth who identified as transgender males. The white matter of their brains more closely resembled that of males.[10]

What does this mean? It means that there is an inherent difference in the brain chemistry of transgender males and females. Trans males and females aren't lying when they say that they "feel" more like a woman or a man. Their brain chemistry shows that they, indeed, have attributes that make them more of a woman or a man, and this has little to do with their reproductive organs.

It was possible that my father's brain chemistry really did mirror that of a female. It was entirely possible that my father was not making this up. My father was not seeking attention or nurturing his ego. In fact, his transition would bring with it profound complications, which would temporarily strip away any sense of personal accolades. My father wasn't transitioning because he was depressed or suffered from anxiety. It was entirely possible that my father suffered from depression *because* of the stress of having brain chemistry that more resembled that of a female while presenting physically as a male, complete with reproductive organs as proof of a male existence. The juggling between brain and body was too much to bear. My father was a trans woman.

I sit in my chair and begin to cry.

My father quietly gets up and joins my wife in the kitchen. My mother and sisters, knowing that I'm not ready to be consoled, get up and join my father and wife in the kitchen. I sit alone in our living room. Later on, I asked my wife what everyone talked about while in the kitchen. "Purses," she replied. "We talked about purses."

Chapter 2

ENTERING THE STORM

Paul Williams was born on May 2, 1951, in Huntington, West Virginia. His father, my grandfather, pastored a small church nearby. Even before his birth, the church played an integral role in my father's life. My grandparents met at a small Christian college in eastern Kentucky, where, at the ripe old age of twenty-three, my father's uncle held the title of president and pastored churches on the weekend. My father had eight cousins on his mother's side, and all but two either went into ministry or married pastors. My grandfather's brothers and sisters, however, grew up in fierce Appalachia. They drank, smoked, fought wars, and sold insurance. My grandfather, the youngest of his siblings, had a different calling than the rough-and-tumble of Appalachia. He pastored churches in Akron, Ohio, and then arrived once again at the doorstep of the small Christian college where he met my grandmother in eastern Kentucky. My father recalls that church and Christianity weren't just passions; they were more like air: "It's what the family breathed."

Being steeped in church tradition meant that my father was expected to fulfill the role of the good preacher's kid and, for the most part, he obliged. Aside from running from the stage right out of the church after a failed attempt at singing "Silent Night" in German, and trying to sneak away and see

Carnal Knowledge at the local movie theater instead of going to Bible study, my father modeled Christian consistency. His life consisted of potlucks and Wednesday night Bible studies. "Singspirations" brought together the congregation so that each attendee had the chance to sing their favorite hymn. There were the church quilts, patchworked by the wise, white-haired women in Akron, and the elders and deacons who kept watch over my father during his formative years in Kentucky. An invitation to see a movie or sporting event on a Wednesday or Sunday would not be considered.

But in my father, there was a rebellious theological streak. My father's ideas about what it meant to be a Christian expanded far past the boundaries set up by his parents. Perhaps it was in response to the unconscious acknowledgment of his female gender identity. Perhaps he recognized that the narrow parameters set forth by the churches where he grew up gave too little room. Regardless, it was time for my father to push open the gates. My father headed to the same Christian college as his parents, but initiated his open rebellion by deciding to pursue a teaching degree rather than one in the ministry.

A few hundred miles away, my mother lived a similar existence. Cathryn Faust was born into a church legacy. My Pop, my mother's father, tells a story of the deep church lineage that started with his great-grandfather, an atheist/agnostic who converted to Christianity and whose children became pastors, starting three different churches. The children of those pastors started four churches. Pop followed in the family business, moving my mother and her three sisters to New York, where they made it their job to start churches. It was their legacy.

My mother and her three sisters toured the country, raising support for churches in New York. They sang about the love of God and how New Yorkers needed that love more than ever. Vacations consisted of performances at various churches and conventions. Life was lived solely for Jesus.

Pop's ministry came equipped with a church on wheels. He'd drive that church up and down the blocks of New York City and Long Island while my mother and her sisters sang in the makeshift chapel on the back of the truck.

My mother inhabited New York but never truly *lived* in New York. Her family considered the largely Catholic makeup of the area to be dangerous, given that "Catholics weren't Christians at all and worthy of damnation." She was so sheltered that she often struggled to pronounce the names of the towns close by. She wasn't allowed to speak with the accent of a native New Yorker, which made the pronunciation of neighborhoods by the natives difficult for her to understand. Her identity was as an Evangelical, working to save the lost souls who prayed the rosary. That same naiveté made its way through each aspect of my mother's life.

My mother remembers school and education being secondary to Evangelicalism. She'd often miss school to go out and sing. Education was only a means to an end; she should go to a Christian college in order to find a minister to marry. Her plans were expedited when my mother saw my father for the first time at a church concert in New York. My father was performing on a tour with the small Christian college choir. She saw my father singing, and decided instantly that this was the man she would marry. He was affable, tall, and good-looking. He went to the same college as her parents. She was sure he'd become a pastor. My mother introduced herself to my father after the concert, and by the time my father left New York a couple of days later, they were dating. My mother graduated from high school on Long Island and made a direct move to eastern Kentucky, where she attended the small Christian college that my father attended, as did his parents before him.

Once there, she hit a snag with her parents' "educational" aspirations for her. Dating Paul Williams meant dating an aspiring history teacher, not the pastor her parents planned for her to marry.

My father's obstinacy threatened my parents' relationship. My mother was bothered by Paul's "liberal" way of thinking and felt very insecure about their relationship.

My mom recalled the disapproval of her relationship with Paul. "My parents made it clear that they did not appreciate certain things Paul said or did. I would constantly argue about religion with Paul before we were married, trying to convince him to believe the 'right' things."

My mother's sisters had no problem marrying preachers. Each fulfilled my Pop's dreams for their lives, and they served at local churches alongside their husbands. My mother took a different path. By virtue of dating a rebellious man, my mother became rebellious by association.

My father eventually conceded his liberal ways and gave up his desire to become a history teacher, instead becoming ordained to ministry, just as his parents and my mother had prayed. They got married and settled into a church ministry in one of Appalachia's poorest towns, where driving to church meant meandering up dry creek beds and canceling the Lord's Day altogether when the rain found its rightful spot in that same creek.

Their patience with flooded creeks wearing thin, my parents took a job in Buffalo, New York, working for a parachurch organization that allowed them to travel, preach, and yes, sing. While my grandparents weren't entirely pleased, their daughter and son-in-law's new course of action was better than the teaching of history, and they indulged their marriage. A few short years later, my father, ever the peacekeeper, moved our family back to the New York City area where, under Pop's tutelage, he began planting churches.

This is my legacy. Both of my grandfathers are pastors. Most of my aunts and uncles are in ministry. Of my eleven cousins, seven of us are currently involved in a ministry. I was born into Evangelical Christianity and church planting. This is my legacy. This is the air I breathe.

And I hate it.

I recall sitting in the front seat of our tan Ford, chafing at both my shirt collar and the agony of defeat. For someone so slight in stature, I have a rather thick neck, and the collars of button-down shirts choke me. I can't wear them. I certainly can't wear them to church. When forced to wear them, I decide that I won't go to church at all. That's what I decide this particular Sunday morning. My mother is in the bathroom, maroon dress on, makeup applied, and a curling iron in her hand. I plead with her to let me wear my second favorite shirt. (My favorite shirt has a giant picture of Fonzie from *Happy Days* giving the defiant thumbs-up, and I know better than to pull that one out of the drawer. But my second-favorite shirt, the one with the cartoon motorcycle, just might be acceptable.) In my five-year-old mind, this is a compromise: a peace offering to my mother that I won't make her Sunday morning routine any more difficult than it needs to be. If I can wear the motorcycle shirt, then I won't complain about having to go to Sunday school. I won't kick and scream my way through children's church, and I definitely won't pick on my younger sisters out of the sheer boredom that comes over me upon hearing the word of the Lord. But my attempt has failed. She hands me a brown polo shirt, and I know that I've lost.

I put the brown polo shirt on and am thankful that its blue stripes make it just dressy enough so that I'm able to honor God with my appearance. At least it's not a button-down. My mom loads up my sisters in the car, and I'm allowed to sit in the front because my dad is out of town. It's a small consolation, knowing that very soon I'll be singing all four verses of six different hymns, picked out and led by the charismatic Jamaican lady.

My dad is preaching at another church in Pennsylvania or Indiana or Oklahoma or wherever he goes most weekends to talk about the Church Planting Mission. It's the church planting organization that Pop started, and my dad goes out to raise money. I know that starting these churches is an important thing, but for the life of me I don't know why.

As my mom pulls out of the driveway I grab at the collar of my polo shirt, gasp, and tell my mom that I'm choking.

A few years later, I'm in the hatchback of a blue Nissan Sentra. It's a far cry from the front seat. I've already missed the first of my two Sunday morning soccer games. I am way behind the skill level of the other kids, the children of the Catholics that my mom steered clear of during her upbringing, who play soccer instead of going to church. My parents reluctantly let me join the team.

I play defense, so I'm the second-to-last one who has any chance to touch the ball. The opposing team needs to get through nine other players before they get to me. The coaches protect me. They know that I'm not up to par. I hide in the back with the goalie and hope the ball comes to me. If it comes to me, I'll stop it. Perhaps a good game today is the beginning of a long and glorious soccer career. My parents will see my talent as God-given, and I'll finally get to skip church for soccer games.

Games on Sunday start at 9:00 a.m., and there's no way my parents will let me play in any of those games. I pray for games that start at 11:00 a.m. or noon—then there's a chance I can go. This Sunday, our first game is at 9:00 and our second at 11:00. My father drives back to Long Island from the church he preached at in Bay Ridge, weaving through traffic on the Belt Parkway. I make it in time for the second game, and I play defense. The ball does come to me, and I give it a feeble kick right back to the other team—the Colts in their cool jerseys—and they score. I see my father on the sidelines. Yes, church is first, but my father is still the rebellious one; the thought crosses my mind that if it were in his power, he'd let me skip church and play soccer every Sunday. But it's not in his power to let me skip church, lest I run out of air to breathe and die.

A few years later, it's me driving the car, and I pull it into a lot across the street from the church on Smithtown Boulevard. My girlfriend has a pack of Marlboro Reds, and we light one up and share it. Her dad is the pastor of the church long ago planted through my Pop's organization. My dad is the director of the Harvest Network. He never liked the name Church Planting Mission, and when my Pop retired, my dad took his place and changed the name.

My girlfriend and I want to shirk our pastor's-kid responsibilities, and I think of three or four excuses we can make so that neither of us has to show up to our Wednesday night meeting. She's doing the same, but we both have a buzz from the cigarette so it takes us too long to retrieve the concocted stories from our psyches. We cross over Smithtown Boulevard and make our way toward the church parking lot.

We cross the street and receive a tongue-lashing from one of the deacons. He's been in our shoes before. He was a wayward teen too, until he was saved by Jesus Christ. "Jonathan, what would your dad think? What would your Pop think?" He immediately pulls out the big guns. I start to smile, and my girlfriend smiles too. We smoke Marlboros behind the bodega because we both care deeply about what our dads think. Word does get back to my father. He asks what I dislike about the church, and then he quietly agrees with me. The church is choking him too.

Not long after, I'm way in the back of my buddy's car; there are nine of us packed into his Chevy Malibu. There's a party, and we know of the only beer distributor in all of Long Island that will sell to minors. My parents left for the National Church Convention, which is somewhere in Indiana, but it's the summer between my senior year of high school and my freshman year of college, and there's no way that I'm missing the last few weeks with my best friends. I walk into the distributor calmly, proudly, and buy a keg.

The cops come while I am throwing up on the back porch. The police get everyone out of the house, and my best friend is smart enough to hide the keg under a sheet in a giant laundry basket. The cops tell me that the way I'll feel tomorrow is punishment enough, and they leave me alone at the house with just my best friend.

I'm glad that my parents are making me go to a Christian college that shares the same values of our church denomination. They told me they'd pay for my tuition only if I went to one of these schools. Anything else and I was on my own. My dad's standing in the denomination ensures that I'll be accepted to one of these colleges, regardless of my academic standing. Thank God for that. While my friends took AP classes to improve their chances of finding a good university, I coasted. Skipping school to go to the beach made way more sense; as an early-accepted student, I made sure I did just well enough to graduate.

I wonder if a relationship with Jesus Christ has never been appealing because all I do is hang out with the Catholic soccer players. My assumption is that when I get to college and all my friends are passionate about Jesus, I'll be passionate about Jesus too. Perhaps for the first time in my life, I'll understand the good news of the gospel that everyone talks about. Maybe I'll know what it means to be saved. Maybe, when I sing the songs at church, I'll get that feeling, the one that causes someone to raise their hands with euphoria at all that God has done. Yes, that'll definitely happen when I get to the Christian college in Tennessee and move away from New York.

I lean against the car and say good-bye to my girlfriend. She's my first love and took the place of my Marlboro-smoking ex. We're going to do the long-distance thing and make it work. I'm sure of it. I start the ten-hour drive down to the Christian college, and I know that everything will change. This will be the point when my legacy makes sense. This is the place where I'll breathe freely. I'll finally find the meaning that has eluded me my entire childhood.

I start decorating my room, and I'm playing my favorite Beastie Boys CD when Doug walks in. He asks what I'm listening to, and I tell him. He shakes his head: Puzzled? Worried? Disappointed?

"You like them?" he asks. "I'm not sure about that message. . . ."

He leaves the room and comes back a few seconds later. He shows me his new CD.

"They're the Christian equivalent of the Beastie Boys," he tells me, and I get sick to my stomach because I know now that, despite all my expectations, I don't belong here. I'm stuck at this Christian college with no way to escape.

I sit in a parked car in a graveyard down the road from my college. My friend passes the joint over, and as I take a pull, I look over my left shoulder to see the police approaching the driver's-side door.

⸺

I tried. I really did. For the first few weeks I even led worship with my new friends who had a band. We sang a song called "Romans 16:19," and we sang it with gusto. I prayed with the guys in my dorm and gamely tried out some of the Christian music they played. I joined a prayer circle and an accountability group.

At every Christian college, there is a group of students that is disaffected for one reason or another. This was my group of friends. Mike was there because his mom worked at the school; he hated all of the God-talk. Dave was secretly gay and had no way to express that at an Evangelical Christian college. John was acting out against his parents' broken marriage. And me? What was I against? Why did I seek these guys out? Why did I give up on church within months of getting to college? I was the rebellious one, just like my dad.

The officer walked up and knocked on the window. He told me to get out of the car, and once I did, he put me in handcuffs. He asked me if I knew why I was being arrested, and I used my right to remain silent.

I felt an overwhelming wave of relief. Utter relief. Holy relief. This transgression would get me away from this place. This school was a daily reminder that I was trapped in a legacy I never wanted, and I breathed deeply as the officer escorted me to the back of the police car.

My transgression came at a tough time for my father's professional career. My father had been receiving offers from big churches and prestigious Evangelical universities. No longer would my dad spend his days in New York. There was the midwestern university, the giant church out west, the church in the Mid-Atlantic. They all had great qualities. They were places of influence. They were places that had the potential to revive the dying spirituality both of my parents were experiencing.

My father had been reading the new "emergent Christian" books. Identified by their progressive theology they challenged the Christian status quo and would soon resurrect my father's liberal ways. I found myself surprised and secretly proud to see Brian McLaren's *More Ready Than You Realize* on our bookshelf during a visit home. He listened to the pastors who challenged the very notion of American Evangelicalism. He went subterrestrial in his studies, knowing fully that anyone who had an inkling of his evolving theological journey could ruin his livelihood.

My mother's faith quietly unraveled with my father's. She distanced herself from her parents and her sisters. Anger burned. She was in the midst of a self-realization that the legacy she inherited from her parents and her parents' parents and their parents brought crippling self-doubt, shame, and an inability to connect with the larger world. My mother was discovering that her legacy was not good news at all, but rather a stifling brand of Christianity. She did her best to hold on. The potential for my father to move forward in ministry and pastor a large church was a last-ditch effort on her journey out of an Evangelical way of living. I

noticed that my mother's rationale for congregational ministry was my rationale for going to a Christian college—they
were last-gasp efforts at maintaining our legacy.

The dalliance my father had with these job offers
marked a greater decision: "Will I stay safe in the relative
confines of traditional Evangelical Christianity or will I
leave the tribe?"

"I knew where my theology was headed," my father
said as we sat on the porch at his home, "and I knew that
it was not compatible with what those churches believed. I
even told them that at [Big Midwest Church], a megachurch
of about four thousand at the time. Integrity mattered."

There was also the matter of the gender dysphoria
that had plagued my dad since childhood. As long as his
professional career continued to soar, my father could
ignore the deep-seated pain of living life as man. "I considered the fact I was trans to be private. I just didn't want
to disrupt the life of my family, so it remained private. And
as long as I thought I'd live my life as a male, it was going
to stay private." For my father, the idea of finally becoming
a megachurch pastor would cover the ongoing pain of his
gender dysphoria. Preaching to thousands of people each
Sunday would keep my father from having to make conscious decisions and assessments surrounding his gender.

But in the end he stayed put, leaving him to journey
out of his tribe alone. Staying put meant that my father's
gender-identity crisis, living just below the surface of his
daily consciousness, announced itself as a force with which
he must reckon. There was no megachurch ministry to
keep it silent.

The spiritual struggles of both my parents inadver-
tently brought me freedom. I too felt unshackled and free
to pursue God in brand-new terms. Maybe I didn't hate my

legacy? While my parents' legacies tormented me, the shedding of those legacies birthed in me the chance to go my own way. The pain of their theological journeys brought a freedom that changed the course of my life. It was possible that my own failures brought with them a new lens with which to see spirituality. With my failure came new beliefs and attitudes, which made my Christian legacy palatable.

College admissions directors, however, were not so elated by my newfound freedom. The red-inked word "expelled" on my transcript made my next move a challenge. In the midst of the frustration came a phone call: "We aren't sure that we can accept you but we want to interview you first." A lifeline.

I showed up at the quaint campus outside of Philadelphia and sat down with the head of the education department. "Your grades aren't good. You've been expelled? Is that correct?" I saw the red ink on the transcript she held in her hand. "Well, at this school we believe in second chances, and we want to give that second chance to you." I thanked her and breathed in deeply. I made arrangements to move to Philadelphia and restart my schooling.

I pursued a teaching degree and, for the first time, outside of the legacy of my family, I was succeeding . . . academically at least.

—

"I don't date white guys," she told me.

I was sitting in the library, reading up on the educational virtues of Erasmus, Horace Mann, and Montessori, when I was approached by a casual acquaintance. I wanted her to become a friend. I wanted her to be more than a friend. She struck up a conversation with me in the library of our school. Later she told me she was procrastinating. She talked to me for three hours. I asked her to join me out one evening, and that's when she told me that she wouldn't date me because of my race.

Jubi is an Indian immigrant. Although she arrived in the U.S. at the relatively young age of two, it was ingrained in her early on that white people didn't share the same values as her Indian kin. "They'll leave you. They'll cheat on you. Their families aren't like our families. They're unpredictable"; the words of her mother and father were still fresh in her mind six weeks after our first date when she told me that our fledgling relationship would no longer work.

"Where my parents are from they can trace families back for generations," she told me. "They know the transgressions of ancestors and make marital decisions based on the health, wealth, and lack of scandal in one's family. They can't do that with your family, and they're never going to change their minds."

"I understand that's part of your culture," I said. "The last thing I want to do is ask you to forsake your culture and adopt mine. If you really don't think this is going to work, then I'll walk away. But if there's any chance that we can be together, then we should fight for us," I said.

My response was gold for anyone who'd grown up on '90s teenage romance movies. It worked, and Jubi told her parents that we were together. As expected, they were devastated. One night, while arguing with her father over our relationship, Jubi told her parents that she loved me and that she was going to marry me. "Love is not a feeling, love is a choice!" her father said. "If you choose to love Jonathan, then you're no longer going to be our daughter."

Jubi's father quickly backtracked on his words, though my future in-laws' fears were not unfounded. In the years they had lived in the U.S., they developed an intimate set of friendships in their South Indian church. No one in their church had ever married outside of their heritage. What would the community say? How would they respond? Would Jubi's parents become outcasts? There was a lot at stake. Regardless of the risks, Jubi was undeterred, and my future in-laws wanted the best for their daughter.

My parents intervened. If Jubi's parents needed to know about family history, wealth, or scandal among generations, my parents would open our family up to that scrutiny. My parents talked about our family's Christian history and its many clergy members. They talked about our family's impeccable background and implicitly assured Jubi's parents that our family would be free of scandal. There were no surprises in my family that might jeopardize Jubi's family in any capacity. My father carried with him his hidden secret. Revealing it would jeopardize my relationship with Jubi and compromise her parents' cultural ethos. But it remained a secret. After a series of conversations, Jubi and I received the blessing we'd waited for.

Three years from the time Jubi used me as a tool for procrastination in the school library, we were married. My father performed part of the wedding ceremony. At the reception, Jubi's father got up to speak: "Love is not a feeling, love is a choice. My daughter chose well."

After getting married, the church we found changed our lives. For the first time, Jesus made sense, maybe too much sense. The liberation theology I studied in grad school afforded me unfettered access to a God who cared more about justice than moral platitudes. The innate rebelliousness that kept me from truly pursuing the family business receded, and the possibility of casting my lot with the rest of the clergy in my family became a concrete option. We prayed with our small group of friends from our church, who had walked with us through the first couple of years of marriage, the struggle of infertility, the long-awaited birth of our first child, and now my vocational unrest. We wondered out loud whether or not our calling was authentic, and Jubi expressed her concern that I was pursuing ministry just because it's my father's chosen profession. I assured her that her assertion was 100 percent true. Yes, we were pursuing ministry in part because it was the family business.

I placed a call to my father, knowing that this call had the potential to tie me to a profession that created an intrinsic familial bond. In ministry, I would live in the shadow of my father. It was a place of comfort and refuge. It was here that I was safe from ever having to challenge my professional capacities. As long as my father was in ministry, I could count on security in my ministerial endeavors and have that same security extend to my wife and growing family.

Paula Responds

I knew that telling my family I was transgender would be extremely difficult for everyone. I had hoped to spare them, but now there was no sparing anyone. I was worried, but our family has always talked things through. When my son refused to meet with me after hearing the news I was transgender, I was distraught. This was not "talking things through." I did not yet understand that some things cannot be talked through; they have to be lived through, and sometimes the first step is to keep one's distance.

I visited New York a few months later, and we sat together in Jonathan's apartment in Brooklyn. He cried hard, as I had not seen him cry since he was a small child. I had badly miscalculated just how devastating this news was.

I had lived with being transgender since I was a young child, three or four maybe. There was not much information available about gender dysphoria during my adolescence and young adult years. Even if there had been, my Evangelical bubble would not have granted me access to it. Fifteen months after we married, I told Cathy what I understood to be true at the time, that I had a cross-dressing paraphilia. I knew that wasn't exactly correct, but I had no word for what I was. It was decades before I knew how to give it a name.

I had never intended to tell my children I was transgender. The only people on earth who knew were Cathy, my therapist, and one trusted friend. A couple of other people knew a little, but not enough to discern a diagnosis. I hid, and I was good at it. I knew if word got out I was transgender, my career was over. I wouldn't even have to transition physically. All I would have to do is come out, and I would lose all of my jobs.

The main reason I did not want to tell the world I was transgender was because I wanted to spare my family the pain. I wanted to get through my life keeping private what I wanted to keep private. But 41 percent of transgender people attempt suicide at some point in their lives, a number nineteen times higher than the population at large. There is no cure for gender dysphoria. It tends to get worse with the passing of time, and some discover that in order to save their lives, they must transition.

I sometimes think I could have made it through life without transitioning, but people close to me feel otherwise. They saw my depression. They lived with it. For me, a lot of those years are a blur. I had spent decades in therapy trying to deal with my gender, and things were getting worse, not better. As the years went by and the struggle became more and more unbearable, I knew something had to be done. The call toward authenticity has all the subtlety of a smoke alarm, and eventually decisions have to be made.

My final decision to come out as transgender was experienced as a call. I was watching my favorite television show of all time, *Lost*. It was the sixth and final season, and there was a point at which the protagonist, Jack, came to realize he had been called by God to die. When I watched that show, I began sobbing and wept as I had never wept before. I knew I had been called.

I screamed at God, "Who the $#%@ do you think you are to have made me this way? Don't you know I'm going to lose everything? Don't you know how my family is going to suffer?" But I knew I had been called, and you reject the call of God at your own peril.

That was in February of 2012. We told the children nine months later.

I did not want to cause pain. I want to empower others, not bring grief into their lives. But the truth is I have brought great grief into the lives of my family members and their spouses and their extended families.

Whenever I speak to people considering transitioning, I always tell them they are very likely to underestimate the impact of their transition on their families. We are a gendered society. We know that the children of gay couples do as well, if not better, than the children of straight couples. But what about when a parent transitions genders? Does a son lose his primary example of what it means to be a man? Do daughters lose the man who protected them? To my knowledge, there have been no studies on how family dynamics are affected by a parent who transitions.

Jonathan had lost his father, the person who had shown him, day in and day out, what it means to be a man. He had gone through the differentiation process that is necessary for all children as they separate from their family of origin, but he carried the memory of a very specific narrative: one in which I was the father and he was the son. I had exploded that narrative, and I had no idea how profoundly that would change the dynamics of our family.

Chapter 3
FAMILY BUSINESS

I carelessly made the twin bed. The mattress was nothing more than a thin layer of foam. Faux log cabins lined the sidewalk, and I could see the lake in the distance. The last corner of the sheet wouldn't fit, and I realized that I was trying to put the sheet on the wrong way. Dave, Derrick, and Scott walked by, and I needed to catch them. The sheet would have to wait. It was my first Harvest Network retreat. My father told me that the retreats were not-to-miss events, regaling us with tales of shenanigans from past retreats. The Harvest guys, the guys whom I already considered family, lived it up at camp. As a teacher prior to my career in ministry, I had spent those September days teaching the volume of a cylinder. But now I was a Harvest Network employee, freed from the bonds of cylinders and ready to unleash my own shenanigans at the retreat.

The Harvest Network was my people, and Dad had told me all about the Harvest guys in our daily phone calls: "Derrick made a bet with Scott and the loser had to get a tattoo! So there's Derrick having lost the bet, getting a tattoo with all of these people looking on. You can't ask for better publicity for your church!" I had never met Derrick, but he was one of my people.

"Someone at Bert's church won the lottery and gave the church all of their winnings." I watched Bert on *Good*

Morning America after that happened. He was funny, a great speaker, and a guy whom I wanted to know.

"Brad is one of the smartest guys in every room. He has more strategic insight in his pinky than most in their entire bodies." I spent extended time with Brad at my first retreat. It was true. The guy was brilliant. He's one of the most encouraging people I know too. Before I worked for the Harvest Network, they were my family. The sheets had to wait. I ran toward the faux log cabins on the sidewalk and caught up with Derrick and Bert. I was home.

My grandfather Charles Faust didn't want to come to New York. Charles figured he could serve the Lord by ministering somewhere in the Midwest. A gruff and ornery gentleman named Elmer Kyle persuaded him otherwise. A trip to New York later sealed the deal. Charles preached in the Bowery, where he noted in his diary that "the trains greatly interrupted [his] preaching every 90 seconds or so." Charles preached to the Jewish folks living in Borough Park and went to Coney Island to "lose his intestines" on the parachute drop and to preach some more. Charles moved to New York with his wife, Penny. They brought two of their four daughters with them. They went to work preaching the gospel for the Church Planting Mission.

Soon after, Charles Faust took over the Church Planting Mission, planting churches in New York with a dream to "evangelize for Christ in ways that no other had done since the days of the apostle Paul!"

By the time I was born, my parents both worked for the Church Planting Mission. Our family lived in a rented house, on a busy street on Long Island in New York, which doubled as the "Mission" office. I lived my earliest years playing with the thimbles on my grandmother's desk, bothering Pop just enough to bring about a welcome distraction. I'd finagle gum from my grandmother, swallow it once the taste wore off, and go back to finagle another piece.

As I got older, I earned four dollars an hour to tie up and bundle the Church Planting Mission newsletter so that it could be shipped across the country to the hundreds of supporting churches. We worshiped each Sunday in Bay Ridge, Jamaica, Greenpoint, and wherever else the Church Planting Mission started a church.

By the time my father took over the Church Planting Mission from Pop and renamed it "The Harvest Network," I was Christian royalty, fully part of a network of churches that Pop and Dad worked to start.

A walk along the retreat path ceremoniously granted me my place in the family business. I served a new church plant on the Upper West Side of Manhattan. My father encouraged our fledgling church to be ahead of the curve. We weren't the normal Harvest Network plant.

Harvest Network churches are planted in the Christian Church / Churches of Christ tradition. Often called the "Restoration Movement," our churches identify themselves by the sacrament of a "believer's baptism" and weekly partaking of Communion. Baptism is the ultimate goal. I was raised with a firm belief that only those who were baptized into the tradition of the Restoration Movement could consider themselves saved from hell. I quizzed my mother one evening as she tucked me into bed: "What about the Methodists or the Pentecostals? Are they saved from hell?" My mother reminded me that it's best to bring others to our churches just so those so-called Christians can be on the safe side, an assertion I now realize my mother never truly believed.

The leadership of my father and his spiritual metamorphosis changed some of the ideology within the Harvest Network, much to the chagrin of other Restoration Movement churches around the country. When my father announced that he had begun attending a Catholic Bible study, I believed him to be a dissident, and yet admired his nonconformity. During his time as a director, he allowed an avant-garde pastor to change the name of his "Christian" church to "Community" church. By forsaking the "Christian" name, my father brought the organization to the brink of extinction; a large number of donating churches pulled their support due to this "heresy."

In one of his final moves as director, my father allowed the hiring of women on staff and in elder positions. He continued to exert his influence as the chair of the board, but he didn't dare address the issue of affirming the LGBTQ community. The affirmation of a community largely deemed by the Christian church as sinful would surely sink the Harvest Network. And so, in accordance with an unwritten policy, any church that declared the LGBTQ community an equitable part of the church would lose the public support of the Harvest Network and the supporting churches within the Restoration Movement.

Armed with the investment from a large Evangelical church in the Midwest, our little church on the Upper West Side pushed the boundaries of the Harvest Network. I accepted the role of associate pastor. Backed by the leadership of my friend and mentor, Jared Witt, our plant was different. While most Harvest Network churches played to the bright lights and big sounds of American Evangelical methodology, we focused deeply on mystery and liturgy.

Yes, Communion happened weekly, but it was a central part of our service, not the afterthought to the praise bands and punchy messages adopted by the Evangelical church. We once again claimed the name *Eucharist*, an homage to high-church worship and a far cry from the more modern and "relatable" terminology of many Harvest Network churches.

Jared—more comfortable citing the psalms of St. Teresa of Ávila than singing along to contemporary worship leader Chris Tomlin—wasn't the typical Harvest Network pastor. Instead of using all of our funds to create church mailers designed to boost worship attendance, Jared created meet-up groups designed to intersect science with faith, sexuality with spirituality, and new atheists with their adversaries. Our church was more interested in good questions than in right answers, and cared more about the number of signups for support of local farmers through Community-Supported Agriculture than about our baptism stats.

Jared was wise to not shake the core of the establishment, however. While friends from the LGBTQ community worshiped and served at our church, Jared made sure it never reached the ears of the big supporting churches using their dollars to keep us afloat in the hope of baptisms to come. Our church plant was free to test the limits of our traditional Evangelical Christianity.

Jared was the completion of my father's newfound Christian ideology, and our church was the hope my father had for his future, in both spiritual ideology and practice. Jared was the leader who could challenge the long-established Evangelical rule of loving the sinner and hating the sin. Jared could carry my father and his church-planting organization to a place where my father's latent gender dysphoria might one day be announced, accepted, and celebrated. I was there to help carry out that legacy. I joined the family business and unknowingly became complicit in shaping a new type of church that had the potential to accept my father as a woman.

It was a vision with which I wanted to agree. I had no map on how to get to the completion of my father's vision, but I knew that if he wanted it, then this was the vision I wanted for our church plant. With Jared's leadership and mentorship in our church, I began seeing the actualization of that vision. It was new, scary, and rebellious—and it failed.

The money from the large churches ran out, and we had no baptisms to bring about a second round of angel investors. The praise of St. Teresa of Ávila didn't match the lure of Chris Tomlin in our predominantly Evangelical denomination.

Our church failed. I failed.

I felt like I had ruined the family business, and more important, I believed that I hurt my father. I wanted our church to work for him. I knew nothing of his secret, but I cared deeply for his ambitious new way of Christianity. I wanted to push the edges that he began pushing in his college years.

I sat at Prime Meats in Carroll Gardens with the founding pastor of a large church in Manhattan, talking through the possibility of a new church plant. We were still in the midst of failure at our old church, and I was thinking through ways we could stay in New York and still have money to survive when this pastor called. His vision was for his church plant to create a daughter church in Brooklyn.

By all accounts, his church was *the* successful Harvest Network church plant. Their baptisms made the Harvest newsletters, and their rising church attendance, even in a place like New York, made them the model all others followed. They were the antithesis of our church on the Upper West Side. This pastor was a church CEO, a strategist, someone who knew exactly how to craft the right message and strike the right chords during worship. His church was everything our old church was not. By even having this conversation, I was certain that I would sell out my convictions and my dad's vision. While our old church pushed against the Evangelical model, this church felt like the shining example of the model itself.

The pastor sat across the booth from me and told me a bit about his own burgeoning progressive theological vision. Perhaps his ideology was compatible? Just to be sure, I called my dad.

My conversation with my father stirred up courage in me; I didn't have to concede my newly developed worship ethos. Yes, it was possible for my father's vision to play out through this church in Brooklyn, and this time I wasn't the associate. I got to call myself the leader. After thorough vetting and some terrible preaching, I was hired for my potential to become a lead pastor.

I hit the road to find a large midwestern church willing to invest hundreds of thousands of dollars in our new church plant, called Forefront Brooklyn. Harvest Network was the primary resource to our church investors. They championed our new church and spoke on our behalf, when hitting the road wasn't an option. Leaning heavily on the help and leadership of the Harvest Network, we raised almost half a million dollars for our new church plant.

The money brought the seed of our church plant. At our inaugural event, I spoke about attending church in Brooklyn. I talked about being home. I talked about continuing a legacy that ran three generations. I talked about how my church family would become their church family. I ordered from Chipotle and talked about the shared meal of the new Christians in the book of Acts. The forty or so of us gathered broke bread with our chicken burritos.

A young woman named Stef Fontela was among those at the table. New to New York, she settled in Brooklyn and stumbled upon our church. We became fast friends, cemented by accepted friend requests on Facebook. Only a few weeks later, while scrolling through friends' photos of last night's entrees and newborns, I happened upon Stef's post: "On national coming out day, I want everyone to know that I'm a lesbian."

I thought about how to respond to Stef's post. Receiving hundreds of thousands in promised dollars has quite the impact on the way we act on our Christian ideals. Stef would be a part of our core team, but she had to know that my publicly affirming her sexuality would mean that the church would fail before it even began. The specter of failure spoke loudly. At the same time, I wasn't ready to return to the cave of illusion from which I'd emerged, so I looked for the in-between. How could I affirm Stef and still start our church? How could I acknowledge her being and still keep the money that our family relied on for survival?

The beauty of social media is the ability to show nominal interest while remaining relatively anonymous. I "liked" her post. It was the perfect way for me to exercise my father's vision disguised as my burgeoning theological beliefs. I kept the spirit of our old church alive. I touched upon my father's vision for a new Harvest Network, and I did it without being noticed by anyone, except Stef.

"I don't think you know what you did when you 'liked' my post," she told me. "I've been shunned by the church. I've been told more often than I can tell you that

I'm loved deeply and yet God can't stand me because of my sexuality. I've been told that I'll never be a part of a faith community unless I keep my sexuality to myself. Your simple 'like' showed me that all of that was a lie. Thank you."

Stef kept a secret—at her expense and for the benefit of our church to be. The secret she kept was that I did affirm her. I affirmed her full being, and I told her that God affirmed her whole being too. I told her about Jared's mentoring and the vision of my father, who desperately wanted a more generous orthodoxy within the Harvest Network. I told her to wait four years before telling anyone else about my father's vision and my illicit thoughts. I told her that in four years our church would be self-supporting, and that we could move on from rules and restrictions to create our own thriving church community that publicly affirmed all.

What I didn't tell Stef was that my grandfather would never approve. What I didn't tell her was that my father was slowly losing influence within the confines of the Harvest Network, and that my father's vision—and therefore my vision—felt further and further from coming to fruition. What I didn't tell her was that, when I do affirm her, I'd ruin a family legacy, and leave the very thing that raised me. I didn't tell her that to affirm her would be to lose a part of myself. I asked to her keep a secret; I pushed my pain and my father's vision four years down the road for the sake of avoiding the specter of failure. Stef kept the secret. Whether she kept it begrudgingly or not she has never said. Asking her to keep this secret for my own security and at her expense is one request that I'll always deeply regret. In my struggle to keep my full self, I took away her full humanity. It wouldn't be the last time a friend and church member would be a casualty of my brokenness.

We raised more funds, gathered monthly to talk about our new community and the ways God was at work in our fledgling group, and served Brooklyn. In September 2012, Forefront Brooklyn Church began with relative success. We had the potential to be featured in newsletters. With the combination of mystery and liturgy I learned from Jared, and the strategy and vision I gleaned from our parent church in Manhattan, Forefront was on its way to accolades.

Just three months later came that phone call from my dad, and suddenly I had my own secret to keep.

"I'm going to tell them soon. I really want to keep working for two more years. I'll take some time to tell them and then ask to stay on for another year." My father told me his plan for coming out in his professional life.

His fingerprints were all over the organization. He was proud of it. The Harvest Network was in his blood. Coming out as transgender jeopardized his status in the organization, and it jeopardized *my* status in the family in far greater ways than my friend Stef's revelation.

My father's proposal to continue at the Harvest Network as an openly trans woman did not afford me the four years I needed to make Forefront Brooklyn financially independent and free to be affirming. It seemed I would have to make a choice; once my father came out to his family at the Harvest Network, I would have to come out too. If I publicly support my father, then this church dies before it even begins.

My decision was an easy one: I didn't want to support my father. I didn't want to help my father come out to anyone. I didn't want to affirm my father. I didn't accept that my father was transgender. My father was mentally unfit, delusional, a megalomaniac. I was angry with my father. I didn't want my livelihood, my career, my ministry, and my family to be affected in any way because of my father's "courage" to come out.

The first year of a church plant is, by far, the hardest work one can do. Pastors talk about routinely working eighty hours a week in that first year to ensure the survival of the church. They serve alongside all of their community members. They listen to the complaints of core members who thought that the new church would finally allow them room to do church their way. They have coffee with, literally, everyone who's ever shown them one iota of interest in being part of a new church community. At the end of the day, a church planter in the first year comes home to spouse and children for the only few minutes that they'll see the family that day. We'll eat, put the kids to bed, only to turn around and walk right back out to meet the folks who want to start a small group. The analogy of spinning plates doesn't come close to the sheer difficulty of leading a startup. My father's transition at such a poignant time in my career felt shameless and unwarranted. How dare my father transition during this time?

I worked to keep my family together. I worked to minister to the new people in our church. And amid it all, I worked to find some middle ground in the conflicting sets of rules about how you are supposed to respond to someone's gender transition. How does one straddle both the popular culture that celebrates gender queerness and the Evangelical Christian church that considers my father to be a sinner in danger of separation from God? I lived in both worlds. Navigating both brought crisis.

"You must be so proud!" my friend texted me upon hearing of my father's transition. Not exactly.

I'm thankful for postmodern culture. In its simplest form, it allows us to see that truth is subjective. It opens us up to new possibilities and accepts new stories. But at its worst, postmodernity accepts each narrative as equally true and equally good. Author Ken Wilbur calls it "aperspectival madness."[1] If every narrative is good and true, then stories have no pain. If every narrative is good and true, then I only have to look for the parts of the story that benefit me.

Popular culture has decided that gender transition is a story of courage and perseverance. It's a good and true narrative, and society is at its best when we applaud those who challenge gender norms. They are featured on magazine covers and in exclusive primetime interviews. TV shows that highlight transgender people are cutting-edge. In our effort to affirm each story as good and true, we invariably dismiss the deeper narrative and the pain that accompanies each story. We know that 41 percent of people dealing with gender-identity crises will attempt to take their own lives. To unequivocally celebrate the experience of being transgender erases the pain and difficulty of gender transformation in order to focus only on the narrative that benefits us. I'm thankful that my friend reached out with his text. But in doing so that friend participated in the aperspectival madness that accompanies my father's narrative. Am I proud of my father? Yes. But I doubt that my friend wants to hear about the years of pain that my father and I went through. It doesn't align with the good and true narrative.

Confiding my father's news with friends outside of the Evangelical world usually meant that they would adhere to the unwritten rule of postmodern culture: "Your father is living out his truth. You should be happy for him." "Wow, it must be really painful for your father to make that choice. How are you supporting him?" My father's public transition a year after his announcement to our family coincided perfectly with the postmodern narrative's newfound affinity for the trans community. My friends often tried to connect back to the source of the courageous cultural narrative, not consciously recognizing that, while these stories benefit them with entertainment and inspiration, they are showing little empathy for the people who actually live out the stories daily: "Have you heard about Caitlin Jenner?" "Do you watch *Transparent* on Netflix?" Well, I've been there and done that with Caitlin Jenner, and I'm living out *Transparent*. I don't need to watch it. I know the pain behind all of the celebrations, courage, and all that is believed to be "good and true."

The rules also state that, while we applaud those courageous enough to go through a gender transition, we spend little if any time talking with their families. The family might tell a different story, one we don't understand and aren't ready to hear. The family might tell a story of navigating the unwritten rules while loving someone who is no longer ours.

Mary Collins laments this reality in her book, *At the Broken Places*, co-written with her trans son, Donald:

> When I spoke about the grief I felt over my "lost" daughter, a counselor told me to keep such thoughts to myself because my transgender son would feel judged. . . .
>
> I know that many transgender individuals face horrible harassment and marginalization, but my

experience with Donald was precisely the opposite. An entire group of people stepped into his new verbal landscape and hugged his new identity with great openness and sincerity. I am now able to feel some semblance of awe at their broadness of spirit, but they went so far down that end of the continuum that they left no space for me.[2]

The postmodern narrative doesn't take into account the sheer complexity of having one's father, brother, sister, mother, child, or spouse become a completely different person on a neurological level. My father told me that his brain receptors responded so positively to estrogen that the doctors marveled; my father was wired to be a woman all along. The synapses and neural pathways of his brain were set to respond in such a way that womanhood affirmed the entire body.

The postmodern narrative doesn't tell you that there are friends and family members whose neural pathways are also literally rewired in the process of comprehending their loved one's transition. What the rules do not allow for are loved ones to process the deep and seemingly bottomless changes that must be made to *our* brains in order to adapt to a new reality. The rules don't tell you that you will experience physical changes to your body in order to adjust to the new reality of having a transgender loved one experiencing changes in their body. That feeling is disorienting; that feeling was not chosen by you but for you.

While I tried to follow the rules of the postmodern narrative, loving my dad and respecting his choice, the dizzying transition that I now faced was one for which I was not even remotely prepared. I knew too well the pain behind the transition, and so the narrative did not benefit me as it might others far away from the daily struggles. Worse yet, I recognized that I took part in the aperspectival madness too. I had participated only in the true-and-good narratives that benefitted me. What I thought was my burgeoning theology of affirmation was nothing more than a nebulous Christian liberalism. I could affirm other LGBTQ+ people, but not my father. Other people fit the narrative better. I wasn't a part of their lives like I was part of my father's. I wanted to honor my father's narrative as good and true, even as it brought pain. Unfortunately, I also lived in a world that still looked poorly on the advent of postmodern culture.

If there are social rules of the postmodern culture, then there are equal and opposite rules in the Evangelical church community. While the postmodern culture sees each narrative as good and true, the Evangelical culture clings tightly to what it sees as objective truth, regardless of individual experience. That objective truth can come only from an "inerrant" reading of the Christian Scriptures, which doesn't look kindly on gender fluidity.

To love someone in the Evangelical world is to tolerate their behavior for a finite amount of time before citing God's wrath to the unrepentant sinner, branding them with a scarlet letter. The purest "love" is that which refuses to leave out the truth. "Love the sinner, hate the sin," and "Always speak the truth in love," the sayings go. To love my father in the Evangelical Christian and professional sense was an implicit rejection of my father's transition and the rules of the postmodern culture. The most difficult of all the cultural and religious navigations came from the people who also "loved" my father. They were disguised as the noble ones who tried to ensure that I played by the Evangelical set of rules, the ones I was bound to by virtue of my church affiliation. They reached out through text and email. They called. They prayed that my father would return to the man whom God made him to be, and I prayed with them.

Good intentions and noble callings are secondary. What the well-intentioned of the Evangelical community wanted for my father and me was secondary to what they wanted for themselves. They wanted to know that their anger was okay. They wanted to know that I wouldn't enforce the postmodern narrative protocol that called for unconditional acceptance, but that I would stand with them in the "love the sinner, hate the sin" ideology. They looked for permission to be confused by my father's transition. They looked for guidance for how to process this news my father had thrust on us all. None of the well-intentioned would ever say my father was damned or living in sin, but they wanted my permission to abstain from affirming him. They wanted me to lead a movement that discredited my father's transition, because they too found the experience dizzying. They asked permission to discredit my father so that they had the chance to keep him. Their good intentions were too much to bear, and yet I refuted none. I listened, offered my impulses, and gave my permission.

Living in the Evangelical realm meant that my father's transition could only be wrong. There were moments when I took a break from my righteous grief and my self-pity; I wanted to join the ranks of the postmodern American culture and fully affirm my father while completely ignoring my grief and the Evangelicals who shared their grief with me. I wanted to applaud her courage and celebrate like everyone else, from afar.

Being caught between two worlds meant that opportunities were limited to communicate the tension of living in both worlds. For both sides, my feelings were fraudulent. I wasn't playing by the rules of either group, but I was living in both. My love and affirmation of my father coupled with my grief and anger toward my father meant that there would be very little honest communication. I needed to wrestle with my dad's transition and postmodern culture along with the Evangelical culture, which accepted only binaries.

My anger couldn't be shared because it would be deemed selfish. It would be deemed callous. It'd be deemed conservative or fundamentalist. If I shared my anger, then it was possible that it would signal renunciation and reversal of all the promises I made to Stef and others in my church that lived in the center of the LGBTQ community. Sharing my anger and grief had the potential to do real damage to the lives of so many longing to be accepted. I couldn't carry that. Acceptance of my father meant the potential for rejection from Evangelicals and the likelihood that our church would suffer an early death. The specter of failure still remained close by after the loss of our first church. Could I really go through that again?

In the complexity of living between the worlds of accepting and unaccepting, I decided that there was another way. I decided to do the work of maintaining my father by remaining firmly in the first stage of grief, denial: My father isn't transgender. My father is still my father, but he's suffering. My dad is still my dad but it's obvious that he's having mental-health issues. My father must have multiple personality disorder. My father is a narcissist. My father wants this change because he's out of touch with reality and is in need of help. I can help my father because—even if my father is mentally unwell, a narcissist, or suffering from a personality disorder—at least he's still my dad. He's still my father. I'm not losing my dad. My dad needs help. To believe this and to pursue this narrative meant that my anger was unnecessary, because no one chooses to get sick; therefore, anger is futile, as it does nothing to cure sickness. I pursued a new narrative that let me keep my dad.

This narrative meant that I didn't have to adhere to the rules of postmodern culture: I don't have to accept my father's transition because he's really not trans. I don't have to live in the judgment of the Evangelical church because my father is battling demons right now. None of this is true, so there's no reason to react to him.

The path of denial made other decisions easier: If my father comes out to the Harvest Network, I do not have to affirm my father, because my father is not transgender. My father is dealing with delusion, and we need to get my father help. That is something that the Harvest Network is good at doing. They are restorers of leaders in the midst of profound struggles. The organization always makes a point of standing by their pastors in crisis. They have walked many a leader through dark nights and restored them back to their churches with needed accountability.

If we can help my father, then he keeps his fingerprints on the vision. Then he just needs to get better, and the Harvest Network can continue onward to bigger things. The rules don't apply here. The rules are only for the people who are really transgender.

If my father comes out to the Harvest Network, our church will not have to affirm the decision, and, in the process, I get to keep my father. That's all I want.

Chapter 4

CRYING IN THE BACK OF A CAB

My father made his transition public, and shortly thereafter, he lost his place within the Harvest Network. Two board members immediately got on a plane to my father's residence where they would pray, attempt to console, and then let my father go. The director called me with a detailed explanation of the consequences of my father's transition. I listened to the man my father hired speak with great pain and anguish at the fact that my father was no longer a part of what we considered family. The director hoped that my father stood in the midst of a mental breakdown, because that could bring restoration. The director often called my father his greatest mentor. He didn't want to lose my father either. I told the director that I loved my father, and he graciously asked no more.

I called my mother, and she told me that Dad's unceremonious dismissal from his organization created a crisis that brought on the greatest kind of despair. Later, my father told me that he sat on both sides of life and death, not certain as to which one would win. My father's closest friend, who supported his transition, flew to be with him in the pain.

I desperately wanted to share in my father's despair but not in the same concerned way of his dearest friend. I wanted to see my father healed, renewed, and repentant.

My father, the one I still longed to be like and to look like, lived in a physically and mentally weak state with which I was completely unfamiliar. The pain of my dad—my strength—becoming weak brought on a depression, which would take years to reconcile.

Deep within the love for my father were impulses—self-righteous impulses—that delighted in my father's pain. His pain caused me pain, and I wanted to punish him for forcing me to share in his struggle. They exposed my anger, coming forth from the depths. My impulses, both dark and difficult to write, exemplify the pain I was still not ready to face.

I had coping mechanisms.

Biju came to visit. He's my brother-in-law, who's not quite related but, within the blurred lines of family, is bound to me as brother. We celebrated my birthday, which should've ended with the first round of Soju shots. The celebration continued through the pitchers of Stella until it was no longer a celebration but the manifestation of a forthcoming funeral. Biju and others in my inner circle became my safe people with whom to mourn. We took a cab down the FDR Expressway, back to my place in Brooklyn. In the cab, I sobbed. I had no breath and no words to describe the purgatory in which I lived with my father and my profession. The alcohol-induced sobbing was enough to frighten the cab driver, who insisted to Biju that we needed to pull over and get it together. Instead, I convinced Biju to join me at the neighborhood bar for one more drink. I buried my head on the bar and continued to weep. Biju asked for us to go home. Alcohol gave me permission to curse my father for being lost. I told Biju we had to stay for one more. I picked up my head long enough to see that we were the last ones in the bar. I took stock of the fact that my grief prevented other patrons from enjoying a peaceful evening, and that it kept the bartender pouring drinks when he longed to go home. I got up and suppressed the anguish, rubbed my eyes, put on my jacket, and stopped crying just before I walked out the door.

My father always knew my business before the rest of the family. My dad was the first one I called with any news. I called my father when, after years of trying, my wife was finally pregnant. I called my father to tell him of my decision to start Forefront Brooklyn on a walk home from the meeting. I hadn't even told my wife. My father led me through the trials of leading a new church startup. He had insight deeper than any other, and it was only his word that could ultimately move me to action. Now my father called me. It had been a month since we'd last spoken. I punished my father for transitioning by slowly and passive-aggressively putting an end to our daily phone calls. I punished my father by not wanting to know her new name. I punished him by refusing to acknowledge her.

"Can I stay at your place a couple of days?" my father asked. "I have some meetings and appointments. Money is tight since I lost my position." My father was coming for a visit for the first time since the announcement of her transition. I had one stipulation. "Please come as Paul." Paul did show up. He was still my father, slightly skinnier, with the effeminate mannerisms generally associated with womanhood, though they seemed fake, like they were unfamiliar even to him. My father curled up on our couch, feet underneath his bottom and arms gesticulating with each word. My father, my hero, my God was a caricature of what he thought to be a woman.

In an effort to understand the transition, my father suggested that I sit down with his counselor. My father's counselor explained to me that those who are transgender will often act and dress in a way that's appropriate to the time they first felt the push to transition. For instance, someone who transitions at the age of fifty might dress and talk in the manner of someone in their teens, due to the fact that they first felt strongly the sense of gender dysphoria in their teen years. "Don't worry," the counselor said. "Your father's affects, dress, and mannerisms are startlingly elegant for someone her age."

To see my father curled up on the couch, pronounced in the need to exert womanhood, felt much the opposite to me. My father, who usually displayed a masculine confidence that I longed to call my own, enacted the presence of a teenage girl, unsure of her burgeoning womanhood and resorting to dramatic gesticulating in order to announce herself as a mature being.

Strangely, my father's unfamiliar body at the same time seemed brave and courageous. His uncertainty felt innate, like puberty all over again. If that's what everyone admired and thought courageous, then I did too. It is indeed a brave decision to leave behind imposing masculinity for something far less familiar and with far less privilege. But my admiration of my father's bravery was met with equal physical disdain. To look at my father was to acknowledge that he was fading, and an obscurity set in that I could not name. This wasn't my father, and yet it was my father. This was my hero, seeming not exactly heroic. I was embarrassed for him.

My father no longer claimed that body. His head and neck, the broad chest, his hands and legs were no longer his. He no longer owned that body. My father's unfamiliar physical assertions posed a question. Through the effeminate characteristics, high-pitched voice, and subtle lisp, I was being asked to no longer claim that body as my dad's either. That body was no longer my indicator of manhood, or what it meant to be *father*. It was no longer the marker that guided my whole life. My father asked me to let that body go. My father sat curled up on the couch before me, and my father was gone. I left and went to check on my kids. I came back out and wept.

"Why?" my father asked.

I stared at our floor for a few seconds. "You're gone." I choked back tears. "You're gone."

Before this, I had never experienced the inability to get out of bed. I'd not experienced the inability to fall asleep. Nor had I experienced the inability to make it through the day without a drink to take the edge off. There is no way to adequately express the fact that my father, who was my absolute center, was fading away in real time. There's no adequate way to express how my father was there to cultivate and guide my very masculine identity, and then to have that very energy, cultivation, and growth taken away completely. I drank to forget the fact that my identity slowly disappeared with my father's. I didn't get out of bed because there was no identity prompting me to create and push on, and certainly no identity that gave me the confidence to lead others.

The weight of each and every revelation and realization—my dad was not coming back to be my dad—sank me deeper. I second-guessed my own heritage. If my father's heritage changed, did mine change with it? According to my father, there was nothing particularly holy about the male body. If that's the case, then was it possible that there was no particular holiness to my body? Was there no importance to my masculinity? To ask each of these questions was to follow it with a drink.

I drunkenly came home one evening yelling, "It's over! It's over."

"What's over?" My wife ran to me.

"The whole damn thing. The whole thing."

I drifted into a fitful sleep, where I dreamed that my father owned a house. In the house lived the friends of my youth, my first love, and a few people I didn't recognize. I opened each door of the house to find where my family would stay. Each room was occupied. There wasn't any more room for me in my father's house.

—

Even as I processed my sense of loss, I created devices that allowed me to cling to the hope of keeping my dad around. Baseball helped bridge the distance.

More particularly, the New York Mets bridged that distance. When I was eight years old, my father surprised me by taking me to my first game. I thought for certain we would go ice-skating in Queens, or maybe we were headed to the 1964 World's Fair. Instead we went to Shea Stadium where I watched a dominant Dwight Gooden strike out seven and lead my Mets to a 4–1 victory. My father and I shared the same passion from that point on. From the highs of the indestructible 1986 Mets to the lows of most of the past thirty years, the Mets were the team that bonded my father and me through my questionable teen years and lost college years. When I became a father, my father accompanied my eight-month-old daughter and me to her first Mets game. Shea Stadium would close, and I wanted her to be there. My father agreed.

My father was no longer my father, but the Mets were the bond I could use to try to keep my dad, my dad. In 2013, the Mets would host the All-Star Game, the first one in the life of our shared passion. I planned to buy tickets and made a rare call to my dad to save the date. I wanted him to come with me to the All-Star Game at the home of the New York Mets. A simulated excitement arose from within my father, perhaps a quick muscle memory of the old normal, "I'll do my best to be there," he said. The easy bond of baseball gave hope to our uneasy relationship. The day drew closer, and I called my father again. My father let me know that he wasn't going to attend the game. He had scheduled a surgery to fix a deviated septum. In the process they would reshape his nose to produce a softer, more effeminate look. My father would miss the All-Star Game at the home of the New York Mets in order to alter his appearance. His body was not equipped to endure the paternal bond that I expected by attending this game together. I no longer cared about my father's body or appearance. The cosmetic changes to his nose represented an entire reshaping of self that I was not invited to know or to comprehend.

I decided that the bond was still mine, and the game still something I deserved. I bought one standing-room-only ticket for $167. My friend Jake and his friend "The Mayor" planned to meet up with me at the game.

I showed up at the ballpark nice and early, bought myself a new Mets cap, and went about the task of looking for meaning or nostalgia or wonder, I'm really not sure exactly. I wanted something that would create a new memory or point to the divine, something redeeming.

Something.

That's when I met "The Mayor."

The Mayor is a lifelong New Yorker, a few years older than me, with a couple extra pounds and a graying goatee. The Mayor was larger than life. Before the game started he confidently told the ushers that we belonged in the first row behind the dugout, even though our tickets said otherwise. The Mayor smiled and talked, and the ushers let us pass. The Mayor took my phone and got pictures of New York Mets All-Star, Matt Harvey, that were so close, one might think he was family. The Mayor yelled with gusto at starting American League pitcher, Max Scherzer. "Max! Max! Max! Max! Max!" When Max Scherzer finally turned around, The Mayor quickly yelled, "Harvey's better than you, Scherzaaahh!!!" and started a "Harvey's Better!" chant that quickly spread to the rest of the ballpark. After the first pitch was thrown, the ushers got wise to our lack of field-level tickets, and we were ushered away from the dugout. It was The Mayor who told us to stand patiently in the players' wives' section of the stadium. "They always leave early. This sh*t bores them. We'll have a seat by the second inning." He was right, and soon we had field-level seats on the third-base line.

It was The Mayor who told everyone to get out of their seats as Mariano Rivera was about to enter the game, "Show some f*ckin' respect!" And then began an epic five-minute standing ovation, complete with laughter, tears, and a thankful acknowledgment of the crowd from a future Hall of Famer. I'll never forget that scene.

I talked baseball with The Mayor throughout. He called me "Pastor," not so much out of reverence, but because he didn't know anyone who "still worked for the Lord."

"Anotha beea, Pastah?" "Pastah, look at the freakin' play that guy made!" And then toward the end of the game, "Pastah, we both live in Brooklyn. Give me a lift home."

I was more than happy to do it. The Mayor made bearable my disappointment of not sharing this game with my father. We left the game and headed toward the Brooklyn Queens Expressway. We laughed about Max Scherzer's face. We marveled at our seats. We listened to sports radio, and made commentary over the commentary. And then my tire went flat.

I pulled off at the closest exit, assuring The Mayor that I'd changed many a tire. I parked on the side of the road, got the spare tire and jack, and told The Mayor that we'd be back on the road in fifteen minutes. The Mayor looked on with doubt. "I nevah owned a car. Nevah needed one. I can't fix that." Turns out, I couldn't fix it either. The car jack wasn't working, and we were stuck on the side of the road, desperate for a good citizen to appear.

It was well after midnight when I took off my new hat to see that it was stained with grease. We sat on the curb with nothing to say. We'd flagged down fifteen—or was it forty-five?—passing cars. Each one greeted us with the same skepticism over our story. Our honesty didn't matter. It was Brooklyn after midnight, and chances could not be taken. Our phones were long dead from trying to get the best in-game photos, and I had let down The Mayor. In some way, I felt like I had also let down my father. He would have had a solution. I did not.

"Ah, Jesus, Pastah, here comes a couple of ladies of the night."

Here they came, two "ladies of the night," decked out in the finest stereotypes one could imagine. They zeroed in on the two of us and made a straight path for the car. The Mayor put his head down, and I took off my hat to inspect it again: "What's going on tonight, boys?"

The Mayor didn't talk, so I told them about the All-Star Game and Max Scherzer. I told them about Mariano

Rivera and my flat tire. I told them about my broken jack, and I told them about my dad, who was supposed to be at the game with me but instead was getting a nose job to hasten the transition of his body to womanhood.

"So you need a jack?" she said. "I know the guy around the corner. We're friends, and he's got a commercial jack. I'll be right back." The two women turned and left.

"Oh God, Pastah! Seriously? Hookahs?" I agreed with The Mayor. What were we doing? There was nowhere to go, and our hopes were set on two women who wanted our money, who very well could have been calling a group to come and rob us, who would continue to define my day more by its disappointments than by a memory. Our hopes were set on two women who approached in the distance towing a commercial jack behind them. It was after 2:00 a.m. when I got back in the car. The Mayor and I said nothing, but nodded in agreement with the sports talk guy on the radio. We turned onto the street where The Mayor would be dropped off. The Mayor finally turned in a way that I had not seen him all night: pensive, contemplative, satisfied.

"Pastah, I think something happened tonight."

"Yeah," I said. "Crazy game and a crazy night."

"Nah, Pastah. Something happened tonight. Something important. Lemme ask you, Pastah. Was God here tonight? I don't go to church, but I think God was here tonight. The game was great, hangin' out with you, but I gotta be honest. I had no faith in those ladies. I think something important happened with those ladies. My mind was changed."

"Like something was there that brought meaning? Like something was redeemed?" I asked.

"Yeah, Pastah! Just like that. Just like that."

My father didn't come with me to the All-Star Game because he was no longer my father. He chose his transition over our bond. It was the lowest point of my transition story, but it wasn't the end of the story.

I called my father. I told him about The Mayor and sitting with the players' wives. I told my dad about Mariano Rivera. My father laughed, wondered, and marveled at the stories. He celebrated the evening with me. My father was no longer my father, but the remnants of a bond remained. It would not break. The worst day of the transition brought forth an inkling of hope that somehow my dad's foray into womanhood was not the end.

So I asked my father her name. "Paula," he said. "It's not that big a deal. It's one stupid letter."

"You don't get to say that!" I countered. "You don't get to say it's one stupid letter. It's an entirely new identity that fundamentally changes your position in the collective consciousness of the entire world! It's not one letter." I paused, "But I'm glad it's Paula. I'm glad it's not, like, Misty or something like that."

My dad didn't go with me to the game, but the game was redeemed, and I believed for the first time that our relationship could be redeemed with it.

Paula Responds

If there is one part of my Christian faith that has never left me, it is my conviction that we really ought to take Jesus seriously when he said the truth would set us free. I have staked my life on it. Humans tend to avoid difficult truth. The pain of denial seems more palatable than going through the hard work of dealing with life in its ultimate reality.

My grandmother was an eastern Kentucky farmer's wife. Though her formal education stopped after elementary school, her wisdom and knowledge were the kind on which you can build a hearty life, grounded in the earth and all of its goodness. What Grandma Stone might have lacked in education she made up for with her common sense and uncommon wisdom. From Grandma, I learned that kindness, gentleness, and mercy were the greatest attributes, and they were grounded in love.

I received a similar message from my father. For forty-five years he was a fundamentalist pastor, though his life never quite matched his theology, which was a good thing. Dad occasionally preached that we were sinners in need of salvation before a righteous God; but he lived as though all people are loved by God just as they are, no strings attached, no changes required. The way in which my grandmother and my father lived was not lost on me.

At the time, I was not all that sure I believed in the existence of any kind of a God in whose image we have been made. There are days I still feel that way. When people ask if I believe in God, I sometimes answer, "Today I do." I've always thought it's all right for me to question God's existence. I think that has something to do with my grandmother and my father. If there was a God, and that God looked anything like the two of them, he or she wouldn't be all that bothered by me questioning his or her existence. Being made of love and all, God has enough grace to be okay with me asking a few troubling questions.

For one, why did God seem so fickle? He (and God was only a "he" in those days) loved me enough to die for me, but had to kill his son to make the whole thing work out for everyone? Hmmm. That just didn't feel right. It did not pass the commonsense test. When any of my three children misbehaved, I never had to punish them before things could be put right with me. Parents do not place their children in harm's way, or send those made in their image to hell.

Though I never quite knew how to approach it biblically, decades ago I came to the conclusion that gay people were as healthy as any other humans. They had loving relationships, their children were healthy, and their character was neither positively nor negatively affected by their sexual identity. The scriptural injunctions against homosexual behavior were few and far between and devoid of a single word from Jesus. I found it odd that Evangelicals became so angry about something never mentioned by Jesus.

For about twenty-five years, I served as a caseworker for several adoption agencies. Some were Christian; some were not. In the early '80s, I placed children with lesbians. The children thrived, as I expected they would. As a caseworker, I had no problem following my conscience. In my church world, however, I was not always allowed to operate with my commonsense-oriented conscience.

I took my cues from my father, who pretty much avoided the teachings of his denomination that didn't square with the gracious person he was. Because I was a well-educated, successful white guy, that approach worked pretty well. People didn't challenge me. I was rewarded with a flourishing career within the Evangelical world. The price I paid for not speaking out boldly in defense of common sense did not become apparent to me until much later. At the time, I opted to function within my tribe, convincing myself I could bring about change from within. I thought that approach was all right. It was not. The LGBTQ population is one of the most at-risk populations in the United States, and the church is one of the main reasons. LGBTQ people cannot serve in leadership in any Evangelical church. According to churchclarity.org, none of the one hundred largest churches in the United States in 2017, as listed by *Outreach Magazine*, were verified as being open and affirming to the LGBTQ population.[1] How could I conclude that continuing to lead in that world was all right? To do so demanded mental gymnastics that were downright ridiculous. We humans are willing to go to great efforts to remain comfortable.

If I had not struggled with my gender identity, I wonder if I ever would have left my comfortable leadership position within the Evangelical world. I would like to think that, eventually, I would have come to my senses, but I honestly do not know.

As it turned out, that choice was not mine to make. Several months after telling Jonathan and our daughters that I was transgender, I told the new CEO of the Harvest Network, and eight days later the board asked me to resign. All my jobs were gone—the megachurches at which I preached, the magazine at which I was an editor, all of it—gone.

After coming out as transgender, I had 65,000 page views on my blog and scores of comments that had to be filtered. I assumed I would be rejected by my denomination, but I did not realize it would be as bad as it was. I thought people would trust that I was a person of moral character and realize they must have been wrong about what it means to be transgender. Instead, most decided they must have been wrong about my character. That was devastating.

It was the beginning of what, to date, has been the most difficult year of my life. It was staggering to lose thousands of friends. Of the thousands of people within my denomination I knew by name, I have heard, in a nice way, from fewer than sixty, have been visited in person by fewer than twenty, and visited more than once by fewer than ten. I have been banished from the church of my childhood, the church in which I built a forty-year career.

What kept me going through that time was the fact that none of my non-Evangelical friends rejected me. Not a single one. You can make of that what you will.

That profound rejection caused me to leave the church, but not my faith. It just caused me to break away from the Evangelical world in which I had resided. I miss my friends terribly, but what I gained has been greater than what I lost.

I gained freedom from doctrines that never passed the commonsense test, and in that freedom came a new understanding of, and appreciation for, the gospel. I did not lose my faith when I transitioned. I found it. I now hold a faith that does not require the suspension of disbelief, deny common sense, or deny the whispering of my heart.

Chapter 5
THE SUPERSTORM

We started our church just a few weeks before Superstorm Sandy, and the joke is that our church has flown in
the midst of that storm ever since. At three weeks old, our
church gathered together hundreds of volunteers to help
repair homes around Brooklyn. Churches from around the
country gave us supplies and money, which we strategically
distributed with the help of our mother church across the
river. We drove generators through a pitch-black down-
town Manhattan. New church members without power
crashed in our apartments. Our three-week-old church
took on a city crisis, and ever since, we've lived squarely in
the midst of that drama.

My coworkers, Ben and Jen, shared in the mutual
victories and the agony of multiple defeats that come with
being church in the midst of a storm. We laughed together
in the sheer exhaustion of the woman who wanted just one
more couch, TV, bookshelf, and serving tray after Sandy
leveled her home. "She thinks our church is a damn fur-
niture store; at what point does it stop?" Jen had no ministry experience, but a quick conversation about her own
shifting theology and her vision for what our church could
be was enough for me to hire her on as our community
director and later our associate pastor. Jen's honesty and

unwillingness to compromise her personality made her an instant fit at our church.

Our worship director, Ben Grace, a transplant from Australia, grew up believing in a cruel God. In this creative role, Ben allowed himself to break free of the old tradition and find new ways to worship a God he was coming to know as far more loving. He wanted to give the exhausted woman all that she asked for and more. That's what love looked like. That's what his God looked like.

Whether appropriate or not, our small staff spent more time with one another and our church community than with our own families. Having already informed the team about the specter of failure lurking around every corner, we worked at a pace that kept the specter at a safe distance, and we didn't let up. The drama continued, and we found our home in the midst of it. Within a few months, our church was thriving. Our collective efforts coupled with our unique backgrounds and skill-sets created genuine excitement in our new community. We grew quickly, and our collective excitement was contagious until it no longer lived only in me.

My dad's coming out just three months after the start of our church intensified the storm in which we already lived. My father announced his transition, and that same night I led our church's first Christmas party. It was supposed to be a celebration of the good that God did for our church in those first few months. I looked out at the hundred-plus people at our party. It was what I prayed for when our church first started: "God, keep the specter of failure away." And that was the case. Here was this tribe, this unlikely group of people, all together with one common goal—to create intimate community in worship—and I was completely hollow. The man whom I wanted to be most proud of our work, the person who spent hours with me on the phone, listening to my missteps and gently pushing me in the right direction, the one who encouraged me to live out our shared vision of a progressive Christian church, told me that he wasn't really a man. He was on his way to live life fully as a woman.

I got up to speak and said something about God's goodness and being a church to rival the community we read about in the book of Acts.

I don't know what I said exactly. Instead, I remember distinctly the chain of thoughts that was going through my head: "If my dad didn't feel like a man but like a woman, and my father was my paternal example, then what does that make me? Am I less of a man too? Am I not the father I thought I was? Is my vision of manhood skewed? I followed my father into the family business, and it wasn't really my father the entire time. It was an imposter. If that's the case, then my even leading this church is fraudulent. I'm an imposter too."

Whether or not there's any credence to those thoughts didn't matter. My initial reaction to my father coming out as transgender was to no longer follow in his footsteps. His footsteps were lies. I thought about resigning on the spot at our Christmas party. Instead I made a few forgettable remarks that belied the crisis beneath.

I'm not sure who said it first, but at some point in the days and weeks following our Christmas party, the staff at both our church and our parent church in Manhattan saw it. Ben called it the thousand-mile stare. He'd say it often, "I know you heard me, but you weren't there, were you?" I wasn't there. I spent the majority of my days looking for clues: "Did I know this was coming? Could I have better prepared myself for this?" The other part of me continually contemplated quitting the church that I just started. My legacy was a lie. This church and our shared vision, all lies. There was no more "like father, like son." And then there was the major concern that maybe it *was* "like father, like son." Perhaps I lived a lie too.

I sat down with the senior leader and founder of our mother church. "You okay?" he asked. "You're checked out, and I'm hearing from a few people that you're drinking too much."

To say anything to him, or anyone on staff, jeopardized my church. It wouldn't allow me the opportunity to straddle two worlds and would force me to choose my father or my Evangelical church. The weight of keeping the secret was physically exhausting. It created a new kind of pressure that I had no business holding.

⁓

At the age of eleven, and in a moment of his own anxiety, my father told me that we didn't have enough money in our bank account for our upcoming trip to Washington, D.C. Aside from my anxiety about whether or not we got to visit D.C. was the greater anxiety that I must help my family make ends meet. I haven't forgotten the weight and helplessness of that fleeting moment. It was the same weight I felt in keeping my father's secret. The weight was bone-crushing, and, much like the moment of great anxiety for my eleven-year-old self, the feeling left me rudderless, with no inkling of how my dad's transition, employment, or our relationship would ever be reconciled. Under the enormity of the secret I could share with no one, I simply checked out of my responsibilities.

I drank to ease that weight. I drank to ease the dizzying experience of physically adjusting to a new reality. I had no energy. What little energy I had was spent just getting out of bed in the morning, and I saved just enough to play with my kids and put them to bed at night. Every other reserve was taken by the secret of my father. Life-changing issues brought to me by my community were better handled with alcohol. I could temporarily forget the weight I carried and give my focus to the new opportunities and relationships of a growing church.

There were real, life-changing problems—big, yet manageable, comprehensible, and ultimately, reconcilable: "I've grown up in the church, but I think that Jesus may be different than the one I know." "I think I'm losing my faith." These issues were to be celebrated, signs of the shift toward the vision my father and I shared to see a different, more gracious, more mysterious, more inclusive Christianity.

And yet I couldn't celebrate these conversations. They drove me into a deeper depression. The good news of the gospel, these glimpses of our vision becoming reality, brought with them reminders that my father would soon cease to exist. That vision went with him.

To feign celebration and to offer spiritual guidance came with a pint glass. With pint glass in hand I could offer hope that people were not losing faith but, in fact, growing in their faith and understanding of the controversial, yet life-giving Christ. I was able to encourage their next steps on the faith journey. I prayed with them and offered new ways forward.

Once the alcohol wore off, I was left with the lonely reminder that *I* wanted to give up the faith journey. I no longer believed in a gracious, life-giving Jesus. The layers of the onion peeled back and revealed that I'd lived off my father's faith all along. My Christian legacy was a lie, just like my father was living a lie.

It's easier to believe the lie while drinking, and so, for the next few months I made sure that there was a pint glass and tap whenever the need arose for me to be pastoral. The consequences would come later, but there was a job to do, and I would do it. Alcohol kept the secret at bay. It kept the lie at bay.

Sunday mornings were the most difficult. The battle felt fierce. It was the same battle, fought weekly with the usual adversaries. The specter of failure from my last church plant showed up each Sunday morning, reminding me that I was only a string of bad Sundays away from failing once again.

After the anxiety of wondering how many people would show up for church, whether or not we had an appropriate worship setting, was the lie that this was my calling. Without the vices afforded to me during the week, and constantly exhausted from battling the host of negative forces, I simply gave up and allowed tears to take over.

A green room behind the stage of our rented theater became my safe space to give up. The green room is where I allowed myself to be soundly defeated. It's where my shoulders heaved, and I grieved the loss of my father and my faith. It was the place where I acknowledged failure as a distinct possibility, and the place where I acknowledged that I had no earthly idea as to what would come next. For years I just assumed that, if all else failed, we'd spend the next couple of months in my parents' furnished basement. That scenario would give us time to get back on our feet and plan our next steps. Surely my father would help us figure out what was next. If the specter of failure ever caught up to us, the security of my family—especially my father—would be the linchpin that kept us safe from a bleak and uncertain future. The basement of my parents' home was no longer a secure place, and my father no longer lived there, but rather, a woman I had yet to meet. The green room was the place I acknowledged that the specter of failure had the upper hand as did the reality that for the first time in my life I was truly on my own.

At 10:55 a.m. each Sunday, the battle came to an end. There were no winners or losers. Some days I came out ahead; some days the secrets, failures, and lies beat me. Regardless, the battle had to end, and Sunday service had to start. I'd dress my wounds, pray a blind prayer, and head outside of the green room to begin greeting our community, cracking jokes, and summoning the energy to truly engage myself in each of those interactions.

For twenty-two minutes in the midst of the service I got to forget about the battle completely. I enjoy storytelling. The Bible, when read in context, gives us some of the most awe-inspiring, violent, loving, controversial, and gracious stories. In the midst of my brokenness, the Bible was more alive than ever, speaking truths to the social and personal structures and dynamics of the day. For twenty-two minutes, I got to tell those stories. For those twenty-two minutes each Sunday, I presented a gracious, loving, compassionate Jesus, who was way more progressive than my father and I could even know. Slowly, that Jesus was becoming my Jesus, and the theological vision that my father and I shared slowly became mine too. The battle shifted in my favor by twenty-two-minute increments each Sunday. Yet I still fought the battles alone. I still carried the burden alone. My father's struggle was still my struggle, and something I could not carry any longer.

Finally, I broke down and told Jen and Ben my secret. There were far too many days they privately wondered why Jonathan, who had been excited and ready to push forward with a bold vision for the church, barely had the energy to make it through a staff meeting. I owed it to them to tell the truth. We came together in the drama of the superstorm, and I needed to confess that more was coming. I needed to be honest enough to let them know that they could decline the next big storm. It was not one I was weathering particularly well.

There was the inevitable shock that happens any time a leader in the Evangelical church decides that he's no longer a man. They knew my father through our Harvest Network connection, and the weight of the secret was not lost on them.

The far more surprising response from Ben and Jen was an inconvenient amusement. They both clearly saw the life-altering power of my secret, but there was also a sense from the both of them that this new truth felt a bit like getting caught in the rain or breaking down on the side of a country road on a beautiful summer day. Sure it had its pain, but with it came a fierce camaraderie that could someday be looked upon fondly. While both Ben and Jen shared in my pain, they carried with it sorely needed levity. They were the first to make jokes. A flubbed announcement at Sunday worship services was often met with, "There are worse things that could happen. Our dads could become women." Their perspective was freeing. They were glimpses that life would go on, and that parts of it were truly good. Their response to the news affirmed the surrealism of the entire scene. They brought a much-needed validation of my absurd thoughts being just that, absurd. The injection of amusement and humor freed me from the graveness I created, and brought me back into the fold of a community I sorely needed. My father's transition was more than just getting caught in the rain, but for the first time my staff empowered me to see beyond what I thought to be a tragedy. The vision of community I preached at our church came to fruition in the form of my staff members reminding me that I didn't have to be alone in my grief. My grief wasn't a lie. It was a challenge. It was the hero's journey, and for the first time I felt that I received the tools for the undertaking. To be freed from the secret of my father's transition was to recognize that there was nothing admirable about carrying that weight in the first place. My journey had companions who could carry the weight with me, for which I'll forever be profoundly grateful. With the weight they carried came the needed laughter. While making fun of Jen during one particular meeting she retorted, "That's a good one. You can keep making fun of me, but just remember that your father's a woman, and that's funnier than anything happening at this office." For the moment it was, and I was thankful.

<hr>

One day, some disaffected members sat down with Ben and me to talk about their unmet expectations. The worship felt exclusive and not accessible, they said. They wondered if the Spirit could even be present in that kind of service. They regretted the fact that their voices hadn't been heard in planning the kind of service that would welcome the Spirit. Ben listened intently, his face reflecting the categorical playback of each service and whether or not our members' concerns held any merit.

He finally spoke, "I'm going to disagree. I think that you're more concerned with your influence being felt in our church than whether or not our worship honors God. I think we're done with this conversation."

It was abrupt, catching both our church members and me off guard. Ben and I walked away from the meeting, and Ben erupted, "You're dad's a f*cking woman, and they're going to bitch about not being able to help with worship? Get your f*cking priorities straight!"

The church members didn't know my struggle. The secret was shared only among the staff members. The church members had no idea about the weight Ben and Jen now carried with me. With the shared information about my father's transition, Ben and Jen also experienced the unwanted overhaul of their gender frameworks. Their jobs were in some ways affected, as they took time to sort through the questions, misgivings, and pain that came with living between their idealized American culture and the far more restrictive Evangelical world, which they both inhabited.

Church members' questions were mostly addressed to Ben and Jen: "I haven't heard from Jonathan about materials for our small group," one person said. Another asked, "Is everything all right with Jonathan? He walked away mid-conversation without even acknowledging that the conversation was over." My staff ran interference. In hindsight, I was completely unaware of how much the staff shouldered my burden. They interceded with leaders or each other to protect our secret. They gave impromptu sermons on acting with grace instead of assuming the worst about their lead pastor. These sermons gave me the space to deal with the pain without people misjudging my struggle as ambivalence or poor leadership. Jen was deft at running interference and making sure the early success of our church would continue. It became part of her job description, another obstacle to starting a church in the midst of a storm.

They were small gestures that, when I reflect on them, brought peace to my life. Jen gently helped me out in my work, encouraging me to shift from personal anxiety to a professional vision. She made me eat and took charge of things for which I didn't need to worry. What I sometimes saw as annoyances were small but powerful tactics meant to refocus my energy to something other than the life of my father.

And when our staff was together, we continued to laugh. The secret kept us in a precarious balance, where any word of my father's transition within our network had the potential to be catastrophic. Under that reality, we laughed, went to the beach, helped each other move, and became a family of our own.

I prayed for the exceptional in our church, and what we received was indeed exceptional. My father's transition was a new development in our denomination, which brought with it a new set of rules by which to be governed and a new set of battles to fight. And with this exceptional challenge came a staff that grew mightily. I found new energy in the camaraderie, the laughter, and in accepting the situation. It was an energy that needed no substance to fuel it, and the need for a pint glass and tap close by dissipated. With the staff sharing in our livelihood, I began to shake the constant need for alcohol. For that I'm thankful.

Later on, after all secrets were revealed and the dust settled, Ben sat down and wrote a song about the storm that continued long after Superstorm Sandy dissipated. It's sung in the style of an Irish drinking song, and it's a crowd-pleaser at church functions. In the "Ballad of Jonathan Williams," Ben penned words that were never truer:

> This is the ballad of Jonathan Williams
> Raised on Long Island a wee Irish lad
> Son of a pastor who then became Paula
> To his shock & surprise now a woman's his dad.

Chapter 6
MEETING PAULA

"Estrangement isn't an option. I think I'm ready to meet my father."

I started therapy about six months after my father's announcement in my living room. Each session, I brought the anger that lived in my gut into the small office along the Hudson River. I was angry that I carried the yoke of his transition through the first year of my church. I was angry at the fact that I had to analyze and reshape my faith on the fly. Of all the anger brought to the surface, none was more painful than the uncertainty of my father's personhood. Who was my father? I rarely saw or spoke to him. I acknowledged my father's new name, Paula, but had yet to see his new body. I'd yet to see the new face, hands, legs, and posture, all of which held her courage and gave Paula her physical personhood.

My sisters, who lived close to my father, saw her often. A text from my sister came through one evening: "You haven't lived until you've seen your dad in women's pajamas." My sisters took Paula shopping and invited her to take part in their children's—her grandchildren's—lives. The grandkids called her "Grandma Paula," a personally frustrating name because of the fact that my sister's children already had a Grandma.

My mother lived full time with another woman, their relationship platonic and incredibly complicated. My mother brought her own resignation to the situation. "Well, you don't throw away forty years of marriage, but I am not a lesbian. I'm not sure what we are, Jonathan."

I was angry for my mother. But the transition was complete for my mother and the rest of my family. To my sisters, Paula was no longer their father. She was simply Paula. I hadn't yet met Paula. My relationship with Paul was strained, but estrangement was not an option.

On Father's Day, my children brought to me a craft beer and a homemade jar of pickles, in my estimation, the perfect Father's Day gift. I thanked my kids. They turned on the Mets game and told me that they'd leave me alone for a while. For Mother's Day, we practically shut down highways, reunite families, and lavish attention on our matriarchs. For Father's Day, we get a beer, pickles, and unfettered access to baseball. That felt about right, and yet my anxiety ballooned.

"Do I need to call my dad today?"

"I don't know. Is he still your dad?"

My wife had her own struggles with my father. My father was something that my wife had never expected or experienced—a tall and imposing white man. She latched on to my father, jokingly calling him "Big Daddy," and delighting in both the generosity and admiration my father showed our family. She had lost my father too, and her tone suggested that, while he was still ours, the pain of calling on Father's Day might be too much to bear.

Our choice not to call ended any hope of getting my father back. There was a new reality, and that reality told me that it was time to wake up from any delusion that I would get my father back. I should give up any hope I had for our past relationship. Any hope I had for hikes, bike rides, or

Mets games with my dad were no more than yearnings for a childhood that once was.

Not calling my dad on Father's Day created a responsibility in me. No longer was I allowed to be passive. I couldn't choose estrangement from him. I wouldn't be the victim of his decision. My decision to not call my father on Father's Day meant that I acknowledged her personhood. I had no father to call, and there was a new person in his place who had also contributed to my very being, who modeled for me the basics of survival, and cared for me in such a way that I might become a well-adjusted human being. The acknowledgment of my father's new humanity felt foreign and contradictory.

I had a choice to make. I could continue to spiral through denial and anger, or I could accept the fact that my father had slowly faded into a nonexistent realm, like the changing of the seasons. In his place was a new person, utterly familiar and yet completely strange but one I must affirm. I could continue to punish my father for her decision to drastically alter her life so late in the game—and in the process profoundly alter my own—or I could acknowledge her personhood. I could acknowledge that my father took a chance and lost everything to become Paula. I could concede that Paula was indeed one of the brave and courageous ones who believed the truth would set her free, even if it came with great pain. If I was willing to acknowledge that, then it was time for me to meet Paula.

I kept my gaze on the homemade afghan in the corner of my therapist's office next to the Hudson River, as I explained the significance of Father's Day: "I'm going to set up a meeting." I walked out of the room before my time was up.

I often judge a moment of my life to be profound based on my body's physical desire to shut down. If I feel like I'm going to pass out, the moment must be important. The time I stole the ball and, in the process, sealed a victory for our basketball team, I tried not to pass out after the intentional foul sent me to the free-throw line. Then there was the game I lost by misreading the game clock. My wedding day, first sermon preached, and when my second child came into the world early. All were moments that I had to will my body not to shut down.

The elevator ride to my father's room could now be counted as one of these profound out-of-body experiences. Paula had flown to New York from her home out west, and was staying at a hotel in the midst of the shops in Midtown. We'd yet to explain Grandpa's transition to our children, and I wanted to meet the person my dad had become first. My wife and I jumped on the train up to Midtown to meet her for lunch.

Paula opened the door, just as nervous, willing *her* body not to shut down. I come by it honestly.

She wasn't my father. Her eyebrows rested neatly above radiant eyes, and a tinge of red highlighted her cheeks. Her nose was no longer pronounced, something I immediately observed. Her mannerisms, which seemed so out of place just a few months ago when my father curled up on our couch, now flowed expectantly and with the grace borne of wisdom and experience. I gave Paula a hug and noticed she'd developed breasts. Paula's hormones were firmly in charge.

"It's good to see you," she said. I had nothing to say back. I couldn't make sense of her voice. There were no masculine overtones and no more evidence of my father's baritone. I searched for any semblance of my father, the mannerisms and the expressions; all of them were gone.

To be devastated and fascinated all at once is rare. The woman before me was not my father. The grief nearly overwhelmed me as I failed to recognize even the slightest bit of my dad. At the same time, I found myself impressed by the woman who sat before me.

"Where did you go?" the therapist had asked me when I stared silently into the afghan. "What if my father is exactly the same but just wearing a dress?" I'd fretted, "What if she doesn't pass as a woman? What if she is dressed in a short skirt with heels and a day's stubble on her face? What if she's wearing some Hello Kitty getup with a lunchbox and the whole damn thing?"

"Then what?" my therapist prodded.

"Then this whole thing gets so much harder. Then I'd be embarrassed to be with my father. My father is my hero, and that feels like a regression. That feels like the people I see on TV. That feels like ladies I've seen walking down Bourbon Street. That's makes the situation that much harder." I was wrong.

Paula navigated the Midtown sidewalks, cluttered with stands of knockoff merchandise, as if she'd taken us to the shops before, moving swiftly between the rack of coats and the salespeople inviting us to check out their new luggage. She wore white pants, a sleeveless blouse, and a pair of flats. Her hair was no longer cut short, but had grown out to expose her natural curls. The men standing outside had one eye on their merchandise, and—I was 100 percent certain—the other stared straight through the woman's exterior and knew her secret as well as I did. I carried her secret, the one she carries every day, through the maze of shops.

I shored myself for comments and even catcalls. My initial reaction was to protect this person who was no longer my father, and yet I was her son. I felt defensive and alert and soon realized I wanted to protect someone I didn't know at all. I tried to stay upright.

The same disruption my body felt upon hearing my father's announcement returned with a vengeance, not because my father looked like the transvestites that walk down Bourbon Street, but because she looked nothing like my father or any other man. Within the well-dressed woman with a tasteful blouse, balanced makeup, new nose, and soft, high-pitched voice was my father. But I couldn't find him, and I thought that might be worse than what I told my therapist.

We sat down to lunch, and the waiter came to take our order.

"Let's start with the ladies first."

By my count there was just my wife and, "Ohhh-hhh, God." Paula ordered something stereotypically befitting of a woman. I took notice of being the only one with fries on my plate. Did my father love French fries? I don't remember, but I'm sure he did, and now she's not eating them.

I remember none of our conversation. I don't remember saying good-bye. I remember thinking that it would take a lot of time to get to know the new person before me—this person who already knows most everything about me. It wasn't fair. Paula had the privilege of having known me my entire life. I met her for the first time in Midtown West, as we navigated second-rate merchandise.

The next day I saw my therapist, who again asked, "Where did you go?"

I had yet to talk, and the afghan seemed close to falling off the back of the chair. I opened my mouth, shut it again, and stared back at my usual spot. My shoulders heaved and tears came, exhausting tears, tears that make an entire body convulse, each muscle contracting and loosening over and over. I put my hand over my eyes and cried for twenty minutes . . . thirty-five minutes? Did I weep for an entire therapy session? I'm sure that I'm not the first. I left having given myself a full-body workout. Every part of me ached, and I stopped at the newsstand for a packet of Advil.

What I couldn't tell my therapist was that my growing up was a lie. Every game of catch in the front yard wasn't with my father. It was with Paula, the woman I just met. When my father lay in bed and read *The Chronicles of Narnia* to me, it wasn't him at all; it was that woman. When my father cheered at school events, or allowed me to accompany him on his church trips, it wasn't my father who supported me. My father wasn't my companion on the trips either. My father never punished me or drove me to the games. It had been Paula dressed in a male costume. She was dressed in drag, and she raised me.

I remembered the bike ride where I learned all about sex. We rode through Heckscher Park for hours, my father carefully explaining parts of the body that he secretly wished not to have and explaining other parts that she wished were hers. My father did not take that ride with me through the park. He didn't teach me about sex. She did. It was her all along.

When my sister locked us out of our car in Hershey, Pennsylvania, my father was furious. We were stuck at Burger King for hours until the police could come and pry open our door. That was the fury of a woman trapped in the body of a man.

When my father spoke at the conferences and told me that I had the gifts to one day speak this way too, it was the nurturing of Paula, a woman I had yet to know: a woman who forced her way into each and every one of my celebrations, defeats, milestones, and intimate thoughts by virtue of disguising herself as a male. It was she who resided in my center and remained in disguise there the entire time. At best, the crisis felt like an episode of Scooby Doo. We pulled off my father's mask to reveal the woman underneath. "I would've gotten away with remaining your father too, if it hadn't been for that pesky truth."

Meeting Paula jarred me. The thought that my father never truly existed was a knockout punch.

I decided that I wasn't ready to get to know Paula. Whether a fair assertion or not, the thought that my father never existed meant that there was no father to call. So I didn't.

I try to liken it to death, but that's not adequate. I told my wife that my dad was gone. I told my dad that he was gone. I mourned the loss of my dad and, whether or not it was fair, I was prepared to talk about grief and loss with anyone in my church community. I believed that I experienced acutely the death of my father. Each new effeminate quality acquired by my father meant a little less of his existence. When my father curled up on the couch in my apartment, I said good-bye to a piece of his existence. With the loss of my father's name, Paul, another huge piece passed away.

It was the idea of my father's transition as death that brought some semblance of closure, or at least its beginnings.

~

With our church continuing its growth, there were new people I was professionally obligated to know. I poured my time into knowing those people instead.

They came with similar stories. The Christianity they knew was no longer a fit. They looked for something that challenged the Scriptures, that included all people from every walk of life, and that allowed each of them space for their questions and doubts. To walk with each of my new friends on their journeys brought satisfaction that the kind of Christianity I talked about on those walks with my dad was taking shape.

My vision for our church was still within the confines of the Harvest Network. My father was let go a few months before I met Paula, and I weathered the storm. We stuck around the Harvest Network because they were still my family. My father might be gone, but this was still my tribe. With the vision of an inclusive church still in my head, I wondered how long it would remain family. But after the realization that it was only Paula who existed, I needed family. I tethered myself to the Harvest Network as my ancestry and my heritage. I reached out to my friends in the organization and did my best to explain to them what happened to Paul. I needed to talk to someone, and it wasn't Paula.

Others sought me out, wondering if I too felt like Paul was gone. A few met Paula, and found the experience equally devastating. Again, they asked for my permission. They wanted to know that it was okay not to befriend Paula. They had the luxury to estrange themselves completely from her; they just needed me to be the one to tell them it was okay to cut the cord. Those with good and noble intentions understood my grief. They too felt Paul's betrayal.

Perhaps I was punishing Paula by attaching myself to those who failed to acknowledge her new existence. Perhaps I was harkening back to a time when I felt cared for, secure, my grandparents in a church office attached to my house.

Grief is mysterious and without rules. Grief is a drug that alters the consciousness and creates in us frenetic decisions that defy any social balance or convention. Grief creates unlikely alliances, and also works to divide the ones whom we love the most.

With my grief firmly in charge, I made the decision that interactions with my sisters and mother were as difficult as interacting with Paula. Grief brought about a temporary estrangement from the family I needed, and directed me back to the ones who quietly, subconsciously, held me accountable to "loving" my father from afar. Grief created new allies whom I already knew would ultimately be a poor fit, unable to accompany me on my journey; and yet grief chose them anyway.

However, in my greatest moments of grief and pain, in all of my estrangement, and in the denial of my father having ever existed, there was another voice. It was a voice that expanded on the fascination I had when meeting Paula. It was a voice that told me to stop looking inward and to stop being the victim. It was a voice that had compassion for my father. It was a voice that told me my father was indeed transgender, that there was no mental instability. There were no major *DSM-5* diagnoses. My father was truly transgender, and for her to come and meet me in the body that she had long ago claimed was indeed brave and courageous.

When my father first announced his transition, he wrote a letter to my sisters and me. In it, he detailed how, at the age of four or five, he firmly believed that there was a gender fairy—kind of like the tooth fairy, I suppose—who would come to him and let him choose whether or not he'd live life as a boy or girl. Once the fairy came, he most definitely would choose to be a girl. That's who he already was. He just needed this entity, this angel, this spirit to come down and acquiesce to his desire. That fairy never came. My father talks about never quite fitting into his skin. There were daily reminders that he was living his false self.

When he met and married my mother, he confessed his leanings to her. Being that they were nineteen and twenty-one, and steeped in a Christian purity culture that said sex and exploration of bodies was a bad thing if it happened before marriage, neither had a clue as to what to do with that information. My parents allowed the struggle to manifest from time to time in ways that I'm not privy to knowing. There were outlets for my father, allowed by my mother, of which I was unaware.

In the letter, my father talked about having children. He wrote that having children made him feel completely and utterly like a father. Being a father was the only time in my dad's life that he wasn't beset by the daily regret of not being able to choose his own gender.

I read my father's letter again and thought about his bouts of depression and anxiety. I thought about the fact that he had a knack for making the smallest of issues into mood-changing events. I thought about how, in the midst of that depression and anxiety, he took the time to make sure that I was encouraged. He took time out to make each one of us feel incredibly special. He took time out to make sure that we were afforded the best experiences that a pastor with a pastor's salary could provide.

Each of my siblings and I had shared experiences with my father that we still treasure. We accompanied my father on business trips where we got to eat at Bob Evans and stay in random hotels in the middle of Ohio. Each Monday was "candy night," when my father encouraged us to get the biggest candy bar and then a little piece of candy for later. Saturdays were for the bacon, egg, and cheese bagels my father brought home. The sandwiches came with our favorite Snapple Ice Teas. He didn't wake us up. It was Saturday, and he knew better than to wake a bunch of teens. He knew what we wanted and picked it up. My father lived his lie, but he lived it selflessly, in the hopes that his children might truly have a father.

Yes, those selfless decisions brought anxiety and depression. They brought the mood swings. They weren't easy. But my father's selflessness brought us a comfortable and happy childhood, filled with myriad experiences that I still celebrate today.

I wasn't ready to get to know Paula, but I felt grateful for her. I was grateful for her because she was indeed my father. Somewhere in the midst of Paula, with her new face, white jeans, and curly hair, was my father. He had the opportunity to make the choice to change genders years before. He didn't, so that we could have a father. As absolutely shocking as it was to meet Paula, there was also a sense that she was finally at peace in her true body. For the first time, there was a freedom in her walk.

My father is tall. I distinctly remember being on a basketball court and imploring my father to dunk a basketball, or at least grab the rim! My father shook his head as if defeated, "I've never been able to do it, Jonathan." What I hear my father saying now is, "I'm sorry. This one's a rental. This is not a body in which I have control or that I particularly want. I can't ask this body to perform great feats. It's not mine."

Paula's body was hers now. It was no longer the rental. She willed it and exerted over it great control. She was in charge. If she was at peace, then it was my turn to make selfless decisions and to get to know Paula so that her life could be filled with experiences of children and grandchildren. It was true. My father was gone. But I stopped wondering if he ever existed. He did exist, willfully, consciously, and with great effort, each and every day of my growing up.

My father's existence was brave, courageous, and selfless. To reflect on my father's selflessness was to have compassion. Reflecting on her selflessness warranted a change within me. While there is pain surrounding my father's transition, it's nothing compared to the pain she endured in striving to be a father. For that I forgave my father, and with that I hoped that she'd forgive me.

Paula Responds

A few weeks after beginning to live full time as Paula, I met Jonathan for the first time. I stayed in Manhattan at a hotel in Chelsea that I knew well and at which I felt comfortable. I wasn't sure staying at their apartment was a good idea. What if things did not go well? Jonathan and Jubi met me at the hotel on a warm September day.

Shortly before they arrived, I began to worry about the stupidest thing. It was after Labor Day, and I was wearing white jeans. You don't wear white after Labor Day in New York. New York has rules. It was one of many things that felt out of season that day.

As well as I thought I knew my son, I could not tell how he was doing. There was small talk, and then we went to lunch at a Mediterranean restaurant up the street. I could not tell you what I ordered and whether or not I ate it. Jubi left shortly after we finished our meal. I thought Jonathan and I might go back to the hotel and talk for a while, or maybe walk down to the Highline and take a stroll. Instead, we walked back to the hotel and Jonathan left, quickly. I thought, "Well, that's not good."

And then I did not see Jonathan for eight months.

Those months were some of the darkest of my life. It was not Jonathan's fault. I had badly underestimated the impact of my transition on those closest to me. The fact that I had lived with the diagnosis for decades did not mean they had. I said to Jonathan, "I'm still the same person." Jonathan said, "No, you're not. You've fundamentally changed." And it was true.

I had always sensed that my brain functioned differently than most males. A study confirmed that reality when neuroscientist Julie Bakker presented results of her functional MRI study of 150 pre-hormonally treated transgender adolescents.[1] The study found that the brain activity patterns of the transgender subjects were very similar to their experienced gender, not their birth gender.

Once hormones have been added, the differences are even greater. The body changes—significantly and obviously. If you transition from male to female, muscle mass shrinks; fat is redistributed; the skin becomes softer and body hair becomes finer. And those are just a few of the physical changes.

Estradiol and testosterone are powerful hormones. The neurological changes do not show, but they are every bit as profound as the other physical changes. They do not appear overnight, but over the course of about three years, the changes touch virtually every part of your being. I was not the same person. I had changed.

During that eight-month period, I had a lot of time to think. I met with a few younger male ministers from my old life. I had been a father figure to a number of them. One said to me, "You really messed with me. You were my only example of an alpha male who was gentle." His words really struck me. Sure enough, I had been an alpha male, and I was gentle. If my transition had been so difficult for a young ministry leader I saw only occasionally, how much more difficult was it for my son? I could not begin to imagine.

I gave Jonathan his space. I had no idea how long it would take him to come back around. On my darker days, I wondered if he would ever come back around.

That first day we met will always be a painful memory. It serves as a reminder of how helpful it would be if they could find the cause of gender dysphoria and cure it before birth. Occasionally I encounter a transgender person who is glad they were made as they were made. I am not one of those people. I would have much preferred living my entire life as a person happy and content in the physical body in which I was born. But that is not my story.

If I had the information then that I have now, what would I have done? It is impossible to know. We make the decisions we make with the information available to us at the time. But this I do know: The call toward authenticity is holy. It is sacred. And it is for the greater good. It was my trust in the fact that the truth sets us free that kept me moving forward through the road of trials, and it is what keeps me moving forward today.

Cathy and my children and their spouses have been on their own roads of trials. They all continue to be gracious and loving toward me, while doing what they must in order to move forward in their lives. All of us keep the company of each other as we can. Our family bond is strong. It has been stretched, but it has not broken.

Chapter 7

AT THE BRIDGE

I was eleven.

"Gramma and Pop are coming over, but you're not going to say hello to them," my mother said. "You're not going to see them. You're going to go to bed. We have to have an adult conversation with them."

My mother walked us up to our rooms to get ready for bed. Gramma and Pop lived close by. We saw Gramma and Pop almost daily. As we got older, we saw them less, but they were an integral part of our lives. Now we weren't even allowed to say hello to our grandparents.

I listened from my upstairs bedroom as my maternal grandparents walked through the door. I listened to the terse greetings. At one point before I drifted off to sleep, I heard someone crying.

We saw my grandparents a few times after that, but it was never the same. A schism occurred between my parents and my grandparents, and their relationship never recovered. Aunts and uncles took sides, which meant that our tightly knit extended family unraveled. The conversation that took place that night affects my sisters and me to this day. While the rest of the family celebrated birthdays and holidays and visited one another over the summer, our family intentionally declined those invitations.

I still don't know the deep struggles of my parents' relationship with my grandparents. What I do know is that I forfeited a relationship with my Gramma and Pop as collateral damage to their conflict. In the time since that meeting, I've been together with all of my family members only three times in twenty years.

My children were six and four. "Where's Grandpa? Why don't we see him?" they asked.

There's no playbook for telling your children that their grandfather is now a woman. There's no playbook for telling your young children that their father is in the middle of a crisis brought about by mourning his father, who is no longer present as a father, but is still alive, and is technically still a father. . . . It gets complicated.

Instead, I told my children about the time that my Pop and Gramma came to visit each of them when they were born. I told them that my grandparents, who now lived in Texas, drove for two days to see them because they loved them deeply. I told them about how I hadn't seen my grandparents for many years before my oldest was born, and that there were times that I missed my Grandpa too. I told my children that they'd see their grandfather soon. I walked out of their room to where my wife was sitting, and announced that my father was coming to visit. "When?" she asked.

I responded that I didn't know. I went on to share with her the conversation I had with our daughters: "Once my parents fought with my grandparents it was pretty much over. We were estranged from my family, and it still bothers me to this day. I won't let the same thing happen to my kids. My father is a wonderful grandparent, and to stop her from seeing the kids because her transition f*cks with our lives is not something I'm willing to do."

Jubi needed no convincing. She missed my father too. I emailed my father and invited her to come to New York. It was time that she met my daughters.

~

John Roebling was the visionary behind the Brooklyn Bridge. The great span that for twenty years held the title of longest bridge in the world connects Brooklyn and Manhattan. It's a magnificent presence along the East River, and brings with it a sense that one has finally made it to New York City.

The bridge had its share of bad luck. Roebling himself never saw the completed bridge. A ferry crushed his foot during the building process, and he died from infection. His son fared slightly better. He contracted the bends from working far beneath the surface of the East River. Unlike his father, he lived to tell the tale. A few days after the opening of the bridge, a rumor quickly spread among the bridge's travelers that a collapse was impending. A stampede commenced, and twelve people died due to the hoax.[1] The Brooklyn Bridge is storied, with an improbable history to match. In 2015, the Brooklyn Bridge marked the place of redemption for my father and me. No bad luck would get in the way. We'd be an exception in the fabled history of the Brooklyn Bridge.

My father flew to New York, got settled, and we took a walk over to the bridge. We found seats at the far side of Pier 2.

Paula's appearance was a punch to the gut. She wore understated yet stylish clothing befitting a woman her age. My father's physical transformation still takes getting used to, and greeting her each time we meet is no

different. The constant question of whether or not I'm
meeting my father, meeting Paula, or meeting someone
else entirely takes my breath away. The fact that I don't
recognize my father in Paula feels like the punch. But this
time, strangely, for the first time since my father sat in a
too-small chair to tell us of her transition, I welcomed her
presence.

At the end of tenth grade, a letter from school was
sent to my home addressed to my parents. With school
finally finished, I was looking forward to going out on my
friend Adam's boat that summer. We'd known each other
since the fourth grade, and he was finally allowed to take the
boat out by himself. We had talked about it at sleepovers for
years. It had only a 40-horsepower motor on the back, but
that was enough to get us to the choice waves over in Fair
Harbor. I got a job sweeping floors at the local convenience
store. Working ten hours a week brought with it a freedom.
The decision about whether or not to purchase fries at the
beach concession stand, or if I could buy the new board
shorts, was mine and mine alone. I was no longer beholden
to the financial leanings of my parents. The tether still connected to my parents and their guidance showed signs of
fraying. This was all by design.

I grabbed my orange smock and broom, and started
sweeping down the candy aisle. My father entered the store
with great intention. My mother rarely sent him anywhere;
he wasn't here to buy milk or to run an errand. My father
walked into the store and toward me with the same intention as he had years earlier, when I picked on my sisters or
gave my mother a hard time.

He walked with the same intention as he had when
I finagled a flight to Virginia to see my cousin. My father
had to pick me up at LaGuardia, definitely not ideal, and I

struggled to keep up as we walked from the airport back to the car and into the New York City traffic.

Now he walked in long strides down the candy aisle. Each time he walked with that intensity, there was always an instant when I thought that he might punch me. He walked down the candy aisle, and I flinched.

"You failed! You failed. That's what the letter says. It says you have to go to summer school. You're grounded for the summer. You won't see anyone all summer."

And that was it. He walked out the door of the convenience store with the same intention as when he walked in. I was left to figure out what I'd failed. I struggled in certain subjects but was wholly confident that I'd studied enough to pass each final exam. I sat in the aisle and thought about whether or not I should steal one of the cream ales sitting in the cooler. The store sold them for 99 cents, and no one bought them. What did they taste like? People on TV always talked about needing a drink, and this seemed like the right time.

Instead, I finished my shift with the sense that things would forever feel different. I had lost my freedom. The tether was secured and tighter than ever. I imagined the fraying.

The next day I went to school to get my summer-school assignment. I walked into the main office, resigned to my fate. No beach or boats, no money, no freedom, and the debilitating anger of my father that made my failure akin to death. I mourned a death, and then the woman in the main office told me I wasn't on the summer-school list.

"Let me get your report card." She left for a few minutes, and it hadn't dawned on me to hope. The intentionality with which my father walked into my job and the authority with which he distributed his punishment left no doubt as to whether or not I'd be in summer school. I didn't believe that my situation could be any different.

"It was a mistake. You passed all of your classes and all of your final exams." The woman in the main office wasn't aware of the severity of my perceived failure and, therefore, didn't feel like an apology was necessary. I went home and told my father that they made a mistake. I showed him my report card, confirming my passing grades and subsequent mistake. I have no recollection as to how he responded, but a taste of freedom was taken from me. I wasn't punished, but the tether remained firmly on my being. This is what I needed to talk to my father about at the Brooklyn Bridge.

I told my father the story. "I was so afraid of that intentionality. I thought you were going to punch me." That shock—the death—still felt real twenty-something years later.

She apologized. "We didn't know what we were doing. I saw your freedom. I saw it. I saw the fact that you were ready to go out and test the world. I saw that you were going to make very different decisions than I ever made. I saw that you would be rebellious. I wanted that. I regretted that I didn't do this."

My father motioned to her body. "This was rebellious. This was what I wanted, and I was confined. You were not. I didn't know how to live with what I wanted, and I regretted it. You never had that problem. I was angry when I thought you failed. I was angry because I couldn't fathom a world with failure. That world compromised the intentionality with which I did life. Failure meant that there was another side. I could not go over to that side."

Paul's survival necessitated intention. Do not search for your freedom; the pain of what you might find is too much to bear. Paul's rebellion took him to the edge but never over, because to fall meant a reckoning with her true self. It wouldn't be too long before I tested limits, swiped cream ales from the cooler, and fell over the edge to find out that death and finality weren't on the other side. I could push limits, find myself, and the world continued to spin. For Paul, to fall over the edge held with it the belief that the world would and should stop spinning.

Paula noticed that the president's helicopters were flying overhead and preparing to land just off of the FDR Drive. Paula mentioned that they were accompanied by the new Osprey copters, and for a brief moment, I saw my dad years earlier, teaching me about helicopters, DC-9s, and L-1011s, the latter a plane with a design flaw that proved fatal one too many times. I was glad as a child not to fly on that plane. I wondered if Paul ever felt so lonely, so confined, that flying on the L-1011 seemed like a chance to take.

She was interested in flight because it scared her. I asked her once why she knew so much about flying machinery. She said, "It's because, when I first started flying, I felt out of control. I learned as much as I could so that I could stay in control of my fear and my emotions."

"Dad, your depression altered our family." She looked out toward the landing Osprey helicopter and apologized.

I found no satisfaction in her apology. I couldn't shake her confinement. I mourned the fact that Paul was never allowed to go beyond the edge. I mourned that she didn't get the chance to swipe cream ales and drink them behind convenience stores. I mourned that she never failed, only to find that the world kept spinning. I mourned for my father the intentionality in which he had to live, even if it did feel like I might get punched in the face.

Her intentionality and depression came from a place of imprisonment. I brought it up for needed closure, and what I found was that for most of her years, my father never got the same peace I asked for at the Brooklyn Bridge. My father had to control everything, down to the specs on a helicopter, to keep the whole thing from falling apart.

During the months we hadn't spoken, Paula had started a blog where she directed a great deal of anger and frustration at the friends of her old life. Her words carried through social media and brought about deep wounds to those considered brothers and sisters in Paul's life. Whether it was willful ignorance or naivety, my father had believed that her friendships would carry through her transition from Paul to Paula. Those friendships didn't carry over. The Evangelical community quickly disposed of Paula, but continued to cling to me.

The intentions of the Evangelical community were admirable and had integrity within the confines of their world. I walked a fine line between living in their world—speaking the truth with love and loving the sinner but not the sin—and a world in which my father's truth was acknowledged and accepted. In my difficult moments and wonderings, I thought of myself as a spoil of a war not yet completed.

Would I end up on my father's side, now clearly on the offensive? Would I remain in the shelter of the old Evangelical community, which still counted my church and me as members? In the meantime, I straddled the line between the warring worlds.

"Dad, I still live and work in your old world. The words that you use to describe the people and institutions with whom you once worked have a direct bearing on my life. With each blog post that talks plainly about your rejection from the Evangelical community, another bridge is burned. With each post, another friendship is irretrievably lost. Are you sure you don't want to extend peace to your old world? Are you sure that you can't extend peace to your old world for my sake? I still live in that place and have to respond to each friend's concerns, feelings, and judgments. Is there another way? Is there another way you can express your frustration? Right now you're angry, and I don't see how it helps either of us to move forward."

I struck a nerve. Since my father's transition, each of her interactions had been measured and gracious, giving me space to grieve and more space to understand the complexity of identifying as a different gender. But this time, her response was not gracious. It was impassioned, and for the first time, I felt an allegiance toward Paula. The winds of this war were shifting: "Do you have any idea what it feels like to show your true self to your best friends and have them completely reject you in a matter of hours? Do you know what it feels like to have your partners in life fly to your city, sit with you in a hotel, and tell you that you're no longer welcomed in their world unless you revert to living a lie? Do you know what that feels like?"

I stared at the bridge. Another tourist boat went by, and someone snapped a photo of my father and me sitting on the pier.

She went on. "Do you know what it feels like to devote your life's work—thirty-plus years—to an organization, only to have them unceremoniously send you on your way once you're vulnerable enough to finally reveal a lifelong struggle?"

My father's tone was even and forceful. This is my father. This is who she is. If Paula had come through the doors of the convenience store to tell me I failed, this is how she would have told me. There wouldn't have been fear, mourning, or intimidation in that conversation. There would have been deep understanding of how very much my father cared and an acknowledgment of the vehement ache she had for my predicament.

"Do you have any idea what it feels like to curl up on a couch after losing nearly everything and deciding whether or not you want to keep on living?" she said. "I write those words because I have to protect myself. My life is at stake. For me to keep the door open for reconciliation is something far more gracious than I can even consider. To invite into another conversation those who hurt me and so quickly rejected my true being means that I'm inviting another attack on my very life. Do you understand that it compromises my ability to survive?"

A man and his daughter stopped to look at the Osprey helicopters that carried our president. My father made small talk with them both, gladly imparting her knowledge of flying machines. I looked at my dad, unrecognizable as my father, and found myself at a personal crossroads. I did rebel. I rebelled against the construct my dad had created to keep it all together. I rebelled against the church. I rebelled against being raised in an Evangelical home and all of the religious platitudes disguised as Christianity. I rebelled against the careful construct my father created that made it difficult for anyone in our family to journey forward in honest exploration of self.

The woman who sat and made small talk around flight finally found the courage to rebel against each carefully crafted ideology. She found the courage to rebel against the construct of the church. She finally rebelled against the moral platitudes disguised as Christianity. She rebelled against the construct and intentionality with which he lived his life so that no one would find her true identity. She even rebelled against her self-imposed limits of personal discovery. She finally went over the edge, and while it was touch and go, the world continued to spin.

I had spent a large portion of two years creating a narrative about my dad's transition to womanhood. My narrative painted Paula as a selfish figure. My narrative portrayed Paula as someone deeply flawed and eager for attention, an extension of the worst I saw in my father. That's not who Paula was. She lived a painful existence, one where she denied herself for the sake of others until she could deny herself no longer. She led an existence that stifled any authentic emotion, which instead manifested in bursts of anger and the need for control. She led an existence that refused rebellion or exploration, which kept her safely in the confines of a life that she did not want. She suffered.

When she decided that she could suffer no more, she lost nearly everything, having to find a way to start over and, literally, risking her life to do so. I couldn't introduce my children to my father without acknowledging that I was wrong to pursue an insurrection against her most authentic being.

To pursue insurrection against Paula was to subconsciously call attention to the fact that something in Paul's life didn't add up. That made sense and was ultimately true.

To pursue insurrection against Paula was to call attention to the fact that something didn't add up in my own life. Yes, my father changed his gender. Yes, I wasn't sure he ever existed. Yes, I didn't recognize the woman in front of me, but I could not introduce her to my children while continuing to revolt against that which was ultimately good and true.

And so, I said, "I apologize. Thanks for taking time to hear me. I want you to know that I hear you too."

My dad relaxed. Her body shifted and became comfortable in a way foreign to me but, I'm sure, second nature to her. We left the Brooklyn Bridge, an exception to its unfortunate history. My father lost it all and was here with me in my city. I was on her side.

Chapter 8

FROM THE MOUTHS OF BABES

When a family member transitions, there is certainly the existential crisis. Second-guessing one's life becomes commonplace. I'd like to think that I wasn't alone in questioning the mental health of my father during her transition. In fact, others who've experienced a loved one's transition will often say the same thing. "Louis" emailed me to let me know that his sister's transition to brother came with certainty that his sister was mentally imbalanced: "How else could I even attempt to explain gender transition?" "Tom" still struggles to know whether his sister isn't suffering from a mental illness far greater than anything derived from her transition.

These are the conversations that we have with others who've experienced the transition of a loved one: "Are they really who they say they are? Are we sure that they're mentally stable?" As Tom likes to say, "We had a f*cked-up childhood. I can't be sure my brother's transition to sister isn't because of the sheer 'f*cked-up-ed-ness' of our situation."

In the stages of grief, family members of those who've transitioned most often have one thing in common; we're very good at denial. We often find myriad possibilities that keep us from having to confront the truth of our loved one's transition. For those who've supported a family member in transition, the other stages of grief are just as real.

Depression, substance abuse, anger, and estrangement are the common threads in the stories of family transition.

As one friend says, "Transition doesn't happen to just one person. Transition happens to the entire family." This is true, but much ambiguity surrounds the ideal way to talk to children about the transition. While everyone agrees that telling children about their transgender family member should be done with honesty, there are way too many wildcards.

One friend tells the story of his transitioning sister adjusting to her new breasts: "These things are sore, and I'm not sure what to do with them yet," she said. His sister continued to talk about her uncomfortable new breasts until my friend's thirteen-year-old daughter chimed in: "You had a choice! I didn't. Now I have breasts that are sore, and I don't know what to do with them either! The only difference is that mine came from puberty!"

My own sister's children have no recollection of "Grandpa." They were not quite three years of age when my dad transitioned, and only know "Grandma Paula." My own daughters loved their grandpa dearly. Grandpa showing up for a visit meant new toys, games, and undivided attention. When told that Grandpa was visiting, both girls immediately ran to their rooms to plan out their day with Grandpa, complete with a visit to Dunkin' Donuts to get Grandpa some tea, and then to the toy store right next door.

The only person who brought equal excitement and anticipation was their Grandma, my mother. Grandma and Grandpa visiting together was akin to winning the lottery. While Grandpa played games and bought toys, Grandma played a game developed over generations throughout my family, the one and only "Mrs. Spinkinackle." Mrs. Spinkinackle combines coloring, acting, deep Long

Island accents, and visits from Mrs. Spinkinackle's dearest friends, all ably voiced and acted by Grandma. Not only is Grandma the master behind the most popular game in the history of my children, she's a teacher, a reading guide, and generally down for whatever comes next. And therein lay the problem.

My children were deeply in love with both Grandma and Grandpa. They had a Grandma, and she couldn't be shared or replaced. On my wife's side, they have an equally important and equally loved Ammachi and Appacha. Grandma and Ammachi were both women with names, cultures, and languages that made them different and special. Appacha and Grandpa were both men, but that changed. Telling our children about the transition felt dizzying before we even broached the subject. What does one tell children who have loved ones going through transition?

Parents and Friends of Lesbians and Gays (PFLAG) is an organization on the forefront of providing constructive ways for families to support their loved ones in gender transition. The PFLAG model calls for an honest yet supportive assessment of family members in transition. For those going through transition, it's of the utmost importance that their humanity is respected. PFLAG gives two specific examples that resonate with my wife and me.

First, when supporting someone in transition, it's wise to be specific and to be confident in the information we want others to understand about our loved one. From PFLAG:

> There is a great amount of pride to be taken in the act of supporting a loved one through a journey that is not universally understood by others. The people around you will follow your lead; the degree to which you can be comfortable (or appear so!) will greatly

influence how those around you respond. Own the words you use, own the confident tone of voice you say them with, and remember that, above all else, you are responsible for acting in the best interests of your [loved one].[1]

My wife and I struggled to understand who my father was and how to best respond to her transition. We also knew that the best thing for our children and for my father was to project the fact that their grandfather would still be the loving and generous grandparent to whom our daughters had become accustomed. Heeding the advice of PFLAG, we thought it best for our kids to start at a place of love and acceptance. They could start from that place only if we modeled it. So model it we did.

We sat our children down and told them that their Grandpa didn't look like their Grandpa any longer. We did our best to explain, "For a long time, even when Grandpa was a little boy the same age as you, he felt like he wanted to be a girl. Even though his body looks like a boy's body, Grandpa has always thought that he has a girl's brain and a girl's heart."

My six-year-old chimed in. "Is that why Grandpa always tells us that we wear pretty clothes and pretty necklaces?" Our children did their best to navigate gender complexity at the ages of six and four.

"Maybe," we said. My wife and I side-glanced and both laughed at the magnitude of what we were trying to tell our children. At points throughout the transition process all one can do is laugh. We continued, "Grandpa has decided that what he looks like on the outside, his clothes, hair, and yes, necklaces will start to look more like how he feels on the inside."

"Grandpa will look more like a girl because that's what he feels on the inside?" My kids were already way better adjusted to this transition than I was.

"Yes. So the next time you see Grandpa, he'll be a girl. He'll be dressed like a girl and have hair like a girl. He'll look different. Grandpa will have a different name. Grandpa's name isn't Paul any longer. Grandpa's name is now Paula." My kids looked equal parts excited and nervous.

It was time to be specific with what we were asking of our children. In telling others about a loved one's transition, the second piece of major advice PFLAG offers is making the specific asks:

> Be clear about what you are asking people to do. Whether it's a request to use a new gender pronoun or new name, to give compliments on new clothes or hairstyles, or simply to refrain from commenting at all, the best-shared stories end with some kind of ask.[2]

We were asking our kids to respect their grandfather's transition by giving her a new grandparent name. We asked our children to talk about their grandfather using female pronouns. We asked the kids to acknowledge the momentous shift in their short lives and to lead with love. The children acquiesced to each of our desires for their new relationship with their grandfather.

Confusion didn't seem to be in the cards. Our children innately understood the gravity of my father's transition and the importance of adhering to new names, pronouns, and gender.

My six-year-old turned quiet. "I think I'm going to miss Grandpa." I started crying. I think my tears brought about more confusion than my father's transition.

"I miss Grandpa too," I said, "but this is what I can promise you. I can promise you that Grandpa will love you the same and play with you the same. Grandpa will still buy you toys and take you to Dunkin' Donuts. Grandpa will still come and see you too!" I couldn't decide whether or not I was reassuring my children or myself. Regardless, both kids perked up and asked about the next visit, which was a couple of days away. "What do we call him? We can't call him Grandma." My older one always put the emphasis on the *ma*, as in, "We can't call him Grandmaaawww."

"What do you want to call Grandpa?" Paula is not their Grandpa any longer. She's still someone who loves them but with whom they're unfamiliar. The memories they had with their Grandpa will eventually feel distant and fractured. They're way too young to remember all of the fun they had with Grandpa. They'll remember some things. They'll remember enough that they'll mourn their grandfather who is still here and coming to visit. While I didn't speak those words to my children, the tears came down my face again as I thought about their navigation through family transitions and the amount of love they had for my dad.

My children projected a quiet strength. For the better part of the day, my six- and four-year-old children were old souls, holding deep the innate knowledge that humanity is often held together by a thread, ready to combust at any moment due to the deep grief and pain of living the inauthentic life. They silently affirmed the changes that would bring new life to their grandfather, and I immediately thought them to have a wise and worldly grace that I myself didn't understand until well into adulthood.

My father and I arrived at our apartment. It is true that we distract ourselves in order to survive profound experiences; otherwise our bodies would shut down from the adrenaline and anxiety. This fact was not lost on my children as they both sat drawing at the dining room table, more so to protect their bodies from overload than to create another refrigerator masterpiece.

Paula walked in, and I watched my children watching their grandfather. Once again, her physical appearance—the curly hair, the curves where none previously existed, the delicately manicured nails and expertly applied makeup—took my breath, and I struggled to maintain awareness as the dizzying effect of my father's appearance once again took hold.

When would I get used to this? If I feel this way, how will the children respond?

Except they didn't respond; they looked at my father and continued to draw whatever it was that stopped their subconscious anxieties from taking over. They didn't run to my father. They stared at their pages. They didn't jump up and yell for Grandpa. It was like they were meeting Santa Claus for the first time. Here's this stranger who knows everything about you. It's intimidating to be completely and utterly known by a stranger, and an imposing one at that.

My four-year-old had already developed a knack for understanding and deftly diffusing tension. She was adept at creating peace among the warring children in her preschool class. Her teacher told us how, upon finding a friend crying in the corner of the classroom, our daughter deferred the attention from the girl's predicament by leading the class in a rousing rendition of "Dynamite" by Taio Cruz: "We gon' light it up like it's dynamite." The dance moves were what really took the children's attention away from their crying classmate.

In a similar move, an argument of the marital kind between my wife and me was ended abruptly by my little one calling out, "I need attention! And by attention I mean clean underpants!"

Her four-year-old mind navigated the complexities of tension and replaced them with timely distractions in the name of keeping peace. Her first encounter with her grandfather would be no different. She looked at her older sister, who wasn't gifted with the same ability to break tension. Our older child sat back and kept drawing, reticent to approach her unfamiliar grandparent. My wife and I, doing our best to remain conscious in the midst of the overwhelming adrenaline surges, were both stuck on repeat. We blankly looked at our children coloring and drawing while robotically imploring our children to greet their grandparent, robotically chanting, "Say hi!" in unintended unison. I'm not sure we were capable of saying anything else, and I'm thankful that no one knocked on our door seeking help at that moment: "My car broke down outside, and I need help!" . . . "Say hi!"

It was time for our youngest daughter to do what she does best, to break the bonds of tension to keep the peace in a moment of great stress. She looked up from her coloring and asked with full confidence, "Grandpa, do you have a penis?"

Our youngest daughter gave us a gift. She deftly mixed her innocent curiosity with the ability to defuse a profound moment hanging in the balance. She knew that her parents proved incapable of defusing the stress. She knew her sister was not equipped.

From the mouths of babes came the question that people often fixate on when rethinking gender identity (though most know—or quickly learn—that it's not polite to ask). She didn't ask in order to get an answer. She asked so that her relationship with her grandfather could begin again, albeit as a new expression.

GrandPaula was the name the children decided upon. After we all laughed deeply at my youngest daughter's successful deflection, after my oldest daughter immediately stood up and went to hug her grandparent, after the tears of thankfulness stopped on my face, and after they took my father to their bedroom to show her their newest press-on nails, they decided that their grandfather's monumental change should be reflected with the name *GrandPaula*.

When seeking advice from PFLAG and other organizations doing the important work of teaching inclusion and acceptance, very rarely do we stumble across suggestions on how to make sure that other family members still feel valued while simultaneously and appropriately respecting the wishes of the loved one going through transition. The best way to honor my father's transition was acknowledge that she was no longer a grandfather. The best way to honor my mother's grace in the midst of transition was to honor her by acknowledging that a name is not just a name. Sharing the name *Grandma* would discredit my mother's role in the lives of my children as much as continuing to acknowledge my father as *Grandpa* would dishonor Paula.

GrandPaula is our attempt to maintain family unity, to acknowledge the importance of those who help raise and care for my children, and to bring respect and acceptance to my father's transition.

It was time for GrandPaula to take the girls for ice cream. The girls had already spent time fiddling with all of GrandPaula's necklaces, which by the sound of the "oohs and aahs" meant that each one was prettier than the one before. They'd played their usual games with GrandPaula. They even went through GrandPaula's bag, knowing that she came bearing gifts given by Grandma, along with a few of her own.

Our youngest daughter's words distracted us from the questions that my wife and I had for our children. Were they afraid of being out in public with GrandPaula? Would they feel the same fierce need to protect GrandPaula that I did during our first visit? Would they pay attention to the possibility of stares and name-calling? When GrandPaula took them swimming, would they worry about whispers around the pool? At what age would they finally and truly understand that their grandfather transitioned to the female gender, and that it's entirely possible that the expression of *grandfather* that they knew wasn't authentic at all? We had questions, and we wanted to sit down and dissect those questions with our children. We wanted to take time and debrief. What kind of emotional toll did their grandfather's transition take on their little hearts and minds?

But these weren't the questions to ask right now. It's possible that they're not the questions we will ever ask. The journey through transition with a loved one is unexampled. We can follow a certain set of principles, but the questions with which we grapple come at different times in different waves. I had been shocked to find out that my father was living full time as a female, which I discovered when my sisters asked my opinion of them taking our father to buy new makeup. I had not been aware that my father was wearing makeup. As it stood, I knew my father's transition to be still forthcoming, and I immediately became emotionally crippled in knowing that my father's transition had already reached a place where my sisters accompanied her on trips to the makeup store. I wasn't ready to respond to that part of my father's journey. My sisters' attempt to debrief their experience backfired in spectacular fashion, and hindered my ability to process my father's true nature. I didn't want to do the same to my children.

There would be a time on their emotional journey when they would have to confront some of their doubts and insecurities. They would grow into an awareness that would lead them to more questions and fewer answers. Those were not ours to expedite.

At the moment, my children were laughing with my father as she showed them the new boots that she had brought them. They were pink, and they were deemed by all to be beautiful. My children put on their new boots and walked out the door because it was time to get ice cream with GrandPaula, and at that point in their journey there was nothing else that mattered.

I walked a healthy distance behind my children and my father. They loved GrandPaula deeply and needed to get to know her. I didn't want to stand in the way of my children getting to know their GrandPaula, and at the same time, I was conscious of the fact that this was only the third time I'd been with my father since her transition.

I struggled with the gnawing feeling that I needed to somehow protect my father. I understood the patriarchy. I objectively knew that my need to protect was rooted in something ingrained in men long before my time. I couldn't shake the feeling that I wasn't so much protecting *her* as I was protecting the fragility of something so new. My father was quite literally born again, and my instinct to protect felt akin to protecting my children as they go out to discover the world. There was purity to my father similar to the earnestness of my children. My wanting to protect my father acknowledged her new birth, her new life, and her new opportunities to interact within her newfound existence. I walked a few yards behind my father and children and simply observed.

A child who's completely secure and comfortable with his or her being will dance. There is rarely rhythm to the dance; nor is there music. The dance can take place anywhere. Spontaneously, a child will begin kicking legs and waving arms to the music that only the child can hear. It's the music of a child who is protected, without harm, and wholly accepted.

At the playground a few weeks prior, I watched as my daughters stood in conversation with one of their peers. In the middle of the conversation and out of sheer delight, one of my daughter's peers started clapping her hands and high stepping. Nothing prompted these movements other than the fact that she was a child fully allowed at that moment to completely live out her childhood. My daughters and the other children had no reaction to her movements. They were all familiar with the dance a child does in the need to express joy.

I watched two other children get in line on a recent trip to Disney World. I, the world-weary adult, weighed the pros and cons of waiting in a line that promised we would be driving a mini-racecar around a track at five miles per hour, within the next ninety minutes. For the two children, the wait didn't matter. All that mattered was the possibility of driving the racecars. The possibility of driving these cars needed some form of physical expression, and so the children danced an awkward and laugh-inducing dance that would end the political career of any adult caught doing so within fifty feet of an iPhone camera. But for the children, the dance was an expression of the unbridled joy they felt living in that particular moment.

I was jealous. I wanted to reclaim dancing as a way to express the satisfaction that comes in the little things. I wanted adults who are in lively conversations to break out in spontaneous dance. I wanted my peers who enjoyed a really good cup of coffee to start stomping their feet and waving their hands. I wanted the anticipation of my next vacation to manifest in jumping up and down, followed by a couple of inspired karate kicks. It's a shame that we have to lose that. At some point, the children will become like us, too afraid to express their joy, self-conscious of the way the world brings about harsh judgments. But for today, our children dance.

My children held my father's hands and they danced. My father's arms swung wildly. She didn't let go as they danced; nor did they want her to let go.

My older child propelled herself forward, jumped, and kicked the air before gravity pulled her back to her GrandPaula. She laughed in the face of gravity and tried again. My younger daughter concentrated on an advanced form of skipping, which seemed to threaten the integrity and structure of my father's arm. Paula didn't seem to care, and neither did my daughter. She soon turned perpendicular to my father and let out a belly laugh.

"That's how God sees my dad," I said out loud. I'm not one to talk to myself, but the words audibly came into being: "That's how God sees my father." I was reborn.

As a pastor, I still struggle with the God of my younger years. That God is separate from God's people. That God is often angry, in search of a better humanity. That God shows grace to the chosen; but that God of my childhood chose only 3 or 4 percent of the world's population. It was up to me to get other people to believe in that God. That God killed his son because that God didn't see me as being worthy. My parents and their parents before me gave that God to me. My father gave that God to me, although I suspect my father only believed in that God to preserve Paul's intentional construction of self. Paul couldn't accept her true self, and, therefore, believed in that God lest it all come crashing down.

I worked hard to shed that God. It took years before I saw the God I know now: mysterious, infinite, unimaginable, and infinitely loving, gracious, and proud of God's creation. It's the God my father taught me in more recent years. She needed this new God for her transition to materialize.

There are moments, before I go on stage to preach, while in a staff meeting with my other pastors, or walking to the subway, that I wonder whether I might be wrong. Do I believe in the wrong God? Is my belief in the infinitely loving Creator off the mark? Perhaps the younger version of my parents and their parents before them were right?

My older daughter started to skip, and my dad broke into a light jog to keep up. My younger daughter continued her belly laugh.

I thought about the God that my father gave me when I was younger. I thought about how that version of God saw no joy in the moment in front of me. That God saw no joy in my children and the sheer surprise and good fortune they felt at seeing their grandparent finally become her true self. In that moment, I buried the old God. If God exists, then God is beside herself with joy at the scene playing out.

The infinitely loving God skipped in front of me. The infinitely loving God continued to laugh and run alongside my father, making sure not to miss a single moment. The infinitely loving God was there in my dad's relief and gratitude over her grandkids. The infinitely loving God couldn't be contained.

My father walked with my daughters to Dunkin' Donuts. I caught up and made my order, completely unaware of whether or not my father passed as woman. I couldn't be bothered with that responsibility. The scene that previously played out was holy. It was a calling to give notice to the God who created every part of my father perfectly.

As I expected, my father bought them one too many donuts. She indulged my children, and they came to expect her indulgence. My older daughter, usually reserved, took a bite of her donut and did the dance. She unleashed a couple of jumps and a twirl, fully confident and wholly loved by her GrandPaula. Repentance didn't come cheaply, and I willingly accepted the energy that implored me to bring this holy experience to others. The old God died with my father, and that was okay. There is a God who sees my father with the same eyes as my children. I accepted the grace of that God—*the* God.

I didn't accept God's grace for my denial or anger. Those still felt righteous, important, and part of making sense of our new reality. I did accept grace for my selfishness. I had made my father's transition a never-ending dark night of my soul with little regard for my father's. I accepted grace because of the ownership I took over my father's story, in the process making it my struggle with body and gender and authenticity. I accepted grace for my assumptions around my wife's parents.

―

My oldest daughter and her cousin played at Ammachi and Appacha's house shortly after my father's visit. They hid in plain sight underneath the black lacquered dining room table. The tablecloth is long enough for a child to feel secure in telling secrets in the makeshift dwelling. My daughter explained to her cousin that her other grandfather was transgender and started living life as a woman. She talked with her cousin about her GrandPaula's visit, and how she missed her Grandpa but still really loved GrandPaula. Her cousin's company saved her from having to silently make sense of her thoughts. Her explanation was for her, not for her cousin—and certainly not for her Ammachi to overhear.

My wife and I had made a decision to wait before telling her parents. Although we'd been together for ten-plus years, the ethos of her Indian immigrant parents rightfully remained entrenched in my wife's consciousness. Their worst fears came true. Jubi married a white man, and the scandal they expected came to fruition. It wasn't the most obvious of indiscretions, but it confirmed her parents' fears.

Jubi remained sensitive to their concerns, regardless of whether or not they were justified. She knew that her parents took on the burden of being the first in their tight-knit Indian community to allow their child to marry outside of their ethnicity. For Jubi's parents to find out about my father's transition meant that they would bear the burden of another scandal.

Upon finding out about my father, her parents would be justified in saying, "We told you so!" That wasn't Jubi's concern as much as the judgments her parents would have to endure from their friends.

My mother-in-law listened intently to my oldest daughter's explanation of her new reality, while she cooked nearby.

Later that evening, she Googled my father's name and confirmed my daughter's secret proclamation and her fears. A couple of weeks later she called my wife.

There's another grace that must be accepted by both my wife and me. There's an underlying guilt just strong enough to manifest in the overzealous need to protect Jubi's parents. The guilt tells us that my wife's parents are not strong enough to endure any worldview outside of their own and must be protected. There is a sense in which Jubi doesn't want to expose her parents to the dominant American culture and its white moral failures. She took on that myth when she married me, but her parents didn't need to enter into that culture.

During my father's transition, Jubi spent much of her time and energy protecting her family from that myth. She suffered with it alone, outside of her ethnicity and upbringing, and, in the process, giving up some of her self.

Jubi's mother called and told Jubi she knew about my father's transition. "I barely knew that man, but I've been crying for two weeks. I'm so sad for Jonathan. Is he okay? I think the kids will be okay. Is he okay though?"

Her parents were exposed to the moral failure. Her parents were right to warn her about me. She now endured the transition and felt the pain that her parents had implored her to avoid. In Jubi's mind, her parents now paid the price for her decision. Her parents' friendships and community were jeopardized once again by Jubi's decision. On her worst days, she felt selfish.

Jubi's mother assuaged the guilt. "Jonathan is family. He's the one I care about. I'm not worried about our friends, Jubi. They're getting old. When you get old, you stop caring about this stuff. I just care about my family."

The grace emanated from my mother-in-law. Her grace gave us another picture of the God who loves unconditionally. Her grace brought with it a confirmation of the wisdom that comes with age and experience.

Her parents' journey brought with it an understanding that life exists outside of their worldview, and that life is worth living too; that life is way better when it reflects the unconditional love mirrored by God.

My wife was free from the anxieties and the myths. She received the gift of grace from her family, and in turn, she accepted the grace that she was not responsible for unwittingly jeopardizing the social and cultural livelihood of her parents.

I saw my mother- and father-in-law a few weeks later. My father-in-law, a man of few words and fewer acts of physical affection, gave me a hug. I sat down at the island that separates the kitchen from the dining room table, while my mother-in-law scanned me for proverbial wounds. She gave me a hug too. "Are you okay? We love you guys. Now eat."

In the moment of accepting God's grace, there was repentance about who my father truly is. We repented of our fear that others couldn't love like my children. We repented of the lies we told ourselves about the ability of others to love unconditionally.

Paula Responds

I had not seen Jonathan since the previous September. It had been a tough eight months. I had not been to church since losing all of my jobs, and I had precious few friends. Most had scattered to the wind. A month after meeting Jonathan for lunch in Midtown, I was contacted by Jen Jepsen, a former member of the Colorado megachurch where I had preached. She heard about my transition and reached out. Today, we are two of three co-pastors at Left Hand Church in Longmont, Colorado. Left Hand is a daughter of Highlands Church in Denver, Denver Community Church, and Forefront Church in Brooklyn, where Jonathan serves as lead pastor. But that is getting ahead of the story.

Jen's friendship meant the world to me. But there was another significant introduction during that season of separation from my son. A friend who had served with me at the Colorado megachurch introduced me to Mark Tidd, the founding pastor of Highlands Church in Denver. Mark and I met in March, and during that first lunch, he invited me to preach at Highlands. It was the beginning of a new life.

Also in March 2015, I made the acquaintance of Jean Hodges, the national president of PFLAG, which gave me an outlet for my energies. I began consulting with PFLAG chapters and lecturing at the University of Colorado at

Boulder, which gave me meaningful work. I was starting to feel like I might have a future.

Jonathan asked if I would come for a visit in May 2015, and thanks to the encouragement of Jen, Mark, and others, I felt strong enough to deal with whatever came. I remember the weather was nice, which is unusual in New York in May. May and June are New York's rainiest months.

I took a cab from LaGuardia to Brooklyn. I had a key that would unlock the basement door to their building, and texted to ask if I should use it. Jonathan texted a single word, "Nope." I didn't know he was home, and was afraid the text meant I would need to remain outside until he got home. Then he texted to say he was in the apartment.

When I went inside, Jonathan was seated at the table with his computer open. He opened the door, and in short order was seated back at the table working on the computer again. But there was a difference in the air, and I knew it was a reconciling difference. I began to silently cry, tears dropping from my cheeks to the wooden floor. I went to the bathroom and got a tissue.

We engaged in small talk, and then Jonathan asked if I wanted to take a walk. We headed down the street, past the junior high, across the pedestrian bridge over the BQE, and down the hill to Atlantic Avenue and New York Harbor. I knew the route. It had been my Brooklyn running route before I transitioned.

We continued past my usual turnaround spot for my 5K run and ended up on steep steps looking out across the East River to the Lower Manhattan Heliport. The Brooklyn Bridge was to our north, casting its afternoon shadow across the steps where we sat.

As we began to talk, three identical Sikorsky helicopters circled the heliport. I told Jonathan that the president was probably on one of them. The Sikorskys were accompanied by Bell Ospreys, a flying machine that can function as both a helicopter and a turboprop airplane. I rarely see Ospreys. They are an anomaly, not quite plane, not quite helicopter. It's how I felt, not quite male, not quite female, forever in a liminal space.

I have little recollection of the specific events we talked about that afternoon. It is the feeling that remains with me, the pain that comes with the work of reconciliation. We've had a lot of talks since I transitioned, and exactly which rocks got moved in that conversation I do not recall. I just remember they were big rocks, the kind it takes two people to move.

By the time Jonathan and I returned from our walk to the bridge, the girls were home from school, and it was time for me to meet them. I told them they could ask any questions they wanted to ask. The girls seemed immediately comfortable, and were not very hesitant. It was clear they had been well prepared for the meeting.

Within thirty seconds, Jonathan's daughter said that yes, she did have a question. She asked, with a giggle, if I still had a particular part of my anatomy. I answered her question, and that was about all the girls wanted to know. We began to play. Later we headed out to dinner, and I held both of their hands as we walked up First Place toward Court Street. I had hope.

I walked them to school the next morning before I headed back to LaGuardia. There was a lightness to my steps and hope in my heart. Maybe the worst was over . . . maybe.

Chapter 9

INCLUSION

The staff sat on the couches surrounding the whiteboard. I'd written something on the board to distract me from what I needed to tell my staff members, who were enduring with me my father's journey and transition. Finally, I said, "We've been holding off for too long. There are too many lives at stake and too many people who've been told that they need to be fixed. We've had too many people who think they're headed to hell, and we're perpetuating these lies."

I told them about my kids and my father. I told the staff that it was time to become a church that wasn't just welcoming but fully inclusive to everyone with a story like my father's. I read this Scripture text from Ephesians 3:16–21:

> I pray that, according to the riches of his glory, he may grant that you may be strengthened in your inner being with power through his Spirit, and that Christ may dwell in your hearts through faith, as you are being rooted and grounded in love. I pray that you may have the power to comprehend, with all the saints, what is the breadth and length and height and depth, and to know the love of Christ that surpasses knowledge, so that you may be filled with all the fullness of God.

Now to him who by the power at work within us is able to accomplish abundantly far more than all we can ask or imagine, to him be glory in the church and in Christ Jesus to all generations, forever and ever. Amen.

We talked about the controversy and fear that was certainly felt when the apostle Paul implored the church at Ephesus to love and include outsiders, the Gentiles. Paul gives a definitive statement to both those on the outside and those tentative to accept them, for them to know "the breadth and length and height and depth" of the love of Christ. This love surpasses anything we think we know or any feelings that would keep us as a church excluding to LGBTQIA persons.

Our worship pastor spoke up first and echoed the sentiment of the staff: "I prayed that we would do this as a church. I've prayed for our church to offer full inclusion of the queer community." The rest of the staff echoed his sentiment and set about dreaming through our church's plan to become fully inclusive to anyone who identified as LGBTQIA.

We knew this would be a challenge . . . we had heard the stories. Churches who decided to affirm the LGBTQIA community lost members. They lost money. Their stories of inclusion threatened the very existence of their churches. Those entrenched in the Evangelical world weren't ready to see certain narratives as good and true. Truth was still objective and given by the Scriptures, which forbade gray areas of gender and sexuality.

Eastlake Community Church was thriving. Their church communities in and around Seattle numbered around five thousand in attendance most Sundays. When a staff member came out as gay, they rallied around her and made a quick decision that the church would give her full support. At the moment of her coming out, they became an inclusive church, but they had yet to tell the congregation. A few weeks later, a *Time* magazine story—meant to highlight the good work of inclusion—unwittingly exposed Eastlake's inclusion without the benefit of walking their congregation through the process.[1] Within months, Eastlake's thriving church community dwindled. They closed locations and let go of staff members.

GracePointe Church outside of Nashville suffered a similar fate. While they had time to announce their affirmation of the LGBTQIA community to their congregation, the Bible-belt culture and its hold on Nashville greatly affected the health of the church. Stan Mitchell, the lead pastor of GracePointe, spoke the biblical language of the Bible-belt culture. He knew better than to stray from the culture's reverence for Scripture, and he talked about the biblical hermeneutic by which he felt compelled to become inclusive. Regardless, the approach left GracePointe struggling to preach the gospel ("good news") of an infinitely loving God.

Doug Pagitt's church in Minneapolis fared a bit better. Doug is considered one of the founders of the "Emergent Church" movement along with the With Collective of progressive churches. Pagitt is the pastor of Solomon's Porch church and shares wisdom around the church's decision to become inclusive: "It's not the smartest growth model," Doug has said to many a pastor; he expands on his thoughts in a *New York Times* article on the subject:

> In mainline churches, clergy tend to be more progressive than their congregations. . . . In evangelical

churches, clergy tend to be more conservative than the people in the pews. And people like it that way. So when the pastor becomes more progressive, that shocks the system. Even people who are themselves O.K. with gay people in churches, something shocks them about their pastor changing. Having that conservative anchor is something they find very freeing.[2]

"Go easy with the congregation," Doug told me. "Make sure the people who were uncomfortable with the change do not feel indicted or unwelcome." Doug's advice was reiterated with each church leader and pastor we met. Part of our plan for inclusivity at Forefront was to visit church leaders who had led their communities through the experience of inclusion. We knew what was at stake.

⁓

Months earlier, shortly after my father's coming out, a friend asked to be baptized. She was introduced to our church through her girlfriend, and found great meaning there. Baptism was significant in our community. With our tagline that we are "a church in search of good questions rather than right answers," we were glad to push the envelope toward love. A handful of queer church members applauded the decision for our friend to be baptized and our willingness to perform the baptism. For me, it was a significant step toward being a church that challenged the Evangelical status quo while still connecting with a key ritual of the Evangelical culture. Our supporting churches loved baptisms. They were a return on investment, the dividends of investing in a new venture. Baptisms were reported to the mother churches with great fanfare and celebration.

Despite my father's transition, I was still hanging onto our old tribe. My father would soon be gone, but I was not ready to follow. I was more than happy to give supporting churches their return in one world while simultaneously celebrating a small step toward affirmation in the life of our friend and the life of our church. I could plant my feet in both worlds without losing all that my father had.

Our baptisms are stories. We celebrate by sharing our story with the rest of the community. Our friend's baptism was no different. On Sunday morning, she stood by the makeshift baptismal we had pulled out of storage a couple of hours earlier. Another church member read her story in front of the baptismal, a symbolic announcement of the celebration to come. The story written by our queer friend started out as an Evangelical's dream. She was a lapsed Catholic. The Catholic Church felt old and stale. She didn't vibe with her priest. She attended Forefront and felt a connection to its style and laid-back demeanor, the ultimate ode to any church practicing the Evangelical methodology.

The dream was short-lived. Not being privy to her story beforehand, I cursed under my breath the sheer ineptitude of my leadership. How could I not have reviewed her statement first? Our friend talked about her girlfriend's role in her faith. She talked about their relationship; she talked about their breakup and reconciliation, and about how she saw God in the nights that she and her girlfriend spent talking. To the Evangelical ear, our friend was "saved" by her girlfriend. The community figured it out. She was gay—and not the repenting kind of gay either. She would be baptized and remain gay!

To my affirming ears, the story was beautiful. It confirmed that we do find the love of God in relationship with others. In no way do we better reflect the nature of the Trinity than when we find God's love in the midst of our most intertwined and meaningful relationships. Our friend's story reflected that; a beautiful gospel message.

But as a leader still living within the Evangelical Christian community, I panicked. This felt like more than just dipping our toes into the progressive waters. Her story sounded more like we were a fully inclusive church, fully immersed in progressive theology. At the particular moment that our friend credited her journey in Christ to her girlfriend, I recognized that my relationship to our tribe might go the way of my father's.

Right on cue, members of our church community stood up in the middle of her story and walked out. The first to stand had attended our church for three months or so. She gave money to our church, and the staff had marveled at the way in which she had jumped into church life. That day, she jumped as swiftly out of our church. We haven't seen her since.

One parent hurriedly left her seat and headed to the children's worship area to pick up her kids. Unfortunately, in order to leave the building, she had to take her children back through the worship area. In the middle of our friend's story, I watched as the same parent rushed out of the building, children in tow. I imagine she was worried her children might hear parts of the story and lose their faith. A few others got up and walked out. Some sent emails explaining their decision to worship elsewhere. One tight-knit group in our church hastily threw together a holiday party for themselves, at which they would decide whether or not to remain at our church. Most left.

My friend's story concluded, and she was baptized.

I mourned for my friend, who certainly watched people get up and walk away, essentially belittling her very existence for the sake of dogma. I mourned the narrative I created in my head in the two minutes between my friend's story and continuing to lead worship. I concocted a worst-case scenario while simultaneously feigning worship: I would lose my tribe and the tradition that came with it. Whether or not it would happen didn't matter. The narrative already came to fruition. I mourned the fact that my friend, a human being, a life, could be only defined by a sexual preference. I mourned the fact that our church community members gave up an entirely satisfying worship experience and a meaningful community over an overly politicized issue.

Our church lost a few members and a bit of financial stability because we baptized a gay woman. Any thought of becoming an affirming church paused, and I temporarily pulled my feet from the waters of progressive theology. I had lost my dad, and I needed my tribe.

On our journey to find our new tribe, we heard the stories of loss from Jenny and Mark at Highlands Church in Denver. Mark told us how he had been asked to leave his position at his previous church for affirming the transgender identity of a young church member. The pain felt by that family, their uncertainty as to whether or not their child could now be loved by God, was enough for Mark to start a new church, fully inclusive from the beginning. There wasn't a transition. In Mark's new church, inclusivity was part of the ethos. Jenny, a co-pastor at Highlands, who had her own coming-out experience, confirmed Mark's sentiment. Jenny asked the tough questions behind our decision to become inclusive; her questions around our accountability as a church for the LGBTQIA community felt like affirmation.

In a phone call and subsequent meetings, Brian McLaren guided us in partnering with our church to provoke curiosity and help our people wrestle with hard questions: "Why is Forefront moving toward inclusion? What is the story of our church, and who are the people that we love dearly? What's their story?" Invoking the curiosity of our church community was the best option for taking the most uncertain community member along for the journey.

Why were we doing this? I told our church about Stef, at this point a stalwart in our church, whose leadership and volunteer work were visible to our entire community: "We have a decision that we have to make. Do we want to be a church that sees Stef lead worship, greet our visitors, hand out Communion, and yet not fully affirm her entire being? Let's have a bigger conversation about an issue that affects the people in our church whom we love the most."

New York is a transient city; many of our church members come from other places across the U.S. Family members nervously sent them to the big city in the hopes that they'd retain the values with which they grew up. Once establishing themselves in the city, their views around LGBTQIA issues changed. As a church member and friend, Sam, told me, "Where I'm from it's easy to have opinions that marginalize the queer population. The majority of people adhere to the traditional Evangelical values of loving the sinner and hating the sin, because they personally don't know anyone who is queer. It's way easier to be against an idea than it is a person. But in New York, you have to share space. Every single day I encounter someone who is queer. They're friends, coworkers, and people with whom I ride on the subway every single day. It's hard to marginalize the same people who you share life with daily."

Regardless, a public shift in values is frightening to the family that stayed behind. My friend went on: "For my family, my public declaration that affirms the queer community reflects not only a loss of values but confirms the anxieties of my family. In their minds, I went to a godless city and became godless."

Brian McLaren encouraged us to invoke the difficult questions as they pertain to family. There will be times when it won't be your church member who needs convincing but your church member's family. Are your members strong enough to publicly go against their family's defined values?

Once again we worked to invoke the curiosity of our church community: "Many of us living in this city work closely with members of the queer community. In fact, many of our friends here at this church are members of the queer community. Is it worth the inevitable questions we get at Christmas and Thanksgiving to stay at our church and support our LGBTQIA siblings?" We created space for the conversations to evoke curiosity.

For the next four months, we communicated to our community with a sense of urgency: "There are members of our church community who are marginalized. There are members of our community who aren't fully accepted as human beings. There are members of our community who are told that, even though God made them in God's image, there is something inherently wrong with their image. As a church, we need to ask ourselves if that's something that we want to continue to perpetuate."

Finally, we told the story of Andy. Andy grew up the son of a conservative pastor. He knew he was gay at age six, and spent the rest of his years working to unlearn his attractions. "God doesn't make people gay," Andy was told, and that's what he worked to rectify.

Andy's parents didn't have to make him go to reparative therapy. His conservative Christian upbringing was enough for Andy to look up the local therapist recommended by Exodus International, a group aimed at "curing homosexuality."

As Andy tells it, "Reparative therapy proposed a number of reasons I might be gay, so I spent many years addressing them all:

> I made sure my dad and I had the best relationship possible, just in case our estrangement had made me gay; I surrounded myself with straight male friends to emulate their masculinity; I dedicated myself to serving the church and to celibacy; I limited my exposure to tempting images and places; and most tragically of all, I limited my emotional attachment to others to ensure love never ensnared me.
>
> I realized I was an empty, unfeeling shell of a human being full of self-hatred and shame that the gospel hadn't worked for me. None of my efforts had made me straight for even one minute of my life, but it had succeeded in killing my faith and love for God. But after years of pursuing a godly life, I was ambivalent about all people and miserable.[3]

We told Andy's story to let our church know that we would soon become inclusive to the LGBTQIA community. We filmed Andy's story so as to not mince any words. Andy talked about growing up in the church and what it meant to hide a part of one's self deep within the church. He talked about what it meant to courageously and anxiously expose oneself, only to receive immediate rejection. He talked about what it felt like to embrace one identity only to lose another.

Andy talked about sharing his heartbreak with friends at Forefront Church and how utterly normal the whole thing felt:

> For the first time, I didn't have to worry about sharing my pain with people who might use it against me later. In his or her eyes I was a child of God in need of care after losing someone dear to me. I wasn't just a gay person. I wasn't someone in need of saving. I was someone in need of reminding that I was created in the image of God and that's what my friends at Forefront did for me. They confirmed that it was okay for me to be gay. It was okay for me to be in a relationship with a person of the same gender. Forefront reminds me over and over that my identity is in God and that I am made perfectly in God's image. As a gay man, I am wholly loved and affirmed by God and by this community.

Andy's video finished, and I made one more attempt to invoke curiosity among our community: "We're going to be a church that affirms the personhood of Andy and anyone who identifies with him. We don't have to be uniform in our thoughts around being gay. But I am asking us what's at stake if we're not unified around the children of God like Andy?"

Unity, and not uniformity, became our church's rallying cry: "We don't have to all agree on the issue of LGBTQIA inclusion; but we can agree that Jesus Christ calls us into affirmation of everyone. In the name of Jesus, our church will begin the practice of full affirmation and inclusion."

More important, Andy's story brought with it a personal and surprising reconversion to Christianity:

> What I didn't expect is for my faith in God to come alive as never before. My resignation from my ordained position of leadership in my church at the time freed me up to find the other gay Christians out there. In the process, I ended up forming a community organization that would help end the isolation of being an LGBTQ Christian. By providing spaces where it's safe to be LGBTQ and Christian, my goal is that everyone who finds our community would rediscover their senses of self-worth as children of God and become resilient in their faith.

I regretted the fact that there were plenty of queer-identifying Christians who passed through our church unable to have their own reconversion experiences. Our church couldn't foster that experience for them.

I thought back to my friend's baptism. She'd since moved out of the city, and I wished she was around to celebrate. I wanted to let her know that I was sorry that I couldn't publicly affirm her sooner.

I thought about the fact that it was time for me to lose my tribe. It was time for me to tell the organization in which I was raised that we were becoming a publicly inclusive church, thus ending my official relationship with them.

That ending had faces and memories. I remembered the time that my family went to a denominational convention in Hershey, Pennsylvania. I played air hockey with my friends, and we ran around the Hershey Lodge, flexing our independence. We rounded the corner back toward the convention hall and nearly ran over an older woman who turned from the Church Planting Mission booth. "You're Charles's grandson and Paul's son, aren't you?" I told the truth and steeled myself for the loss of independence that comes from almost knocking over an elderly woman. "Bless you and your family," she said. She rooted around her purse and handed me a Hershey Kiss. "I pray you keep up the good work."

—

My wife makes cheese plates and crudités when she's anxious about having guests. Her first impressions are made with a wide array of hors d'oeuvres. If our close friends are coming over, then it's a potluck. The pressure is off and there's no need for Havarti with grapes or the full salami plate. This particular evening challenged Jubi. Our good friends from the Harvest Network were coming over to have a Matthew 18 moment with us.

> If another member of the church sins against you, go and point out the fault when the two of you are alone. If the member listens to you, you have regained that one. But if you are not listened to, take one or two others along with you, so that every word may be confirmed by the evidence of two or three witnesses. If the member refuses to listen to them, tell it to the church; and if the offender refuses to listen even to the church, let such a one be to you as a Gentile and a tax collector. (Matt. 18:15–17)

Another couple from our church would join them, to make the Matthew 18 delegation complete. What does one put out as appetizers when joined by friends who believe you to be misleading a church? My friend said,

> Jonathan, we think that there are many ways that you're gifted, but we believe that the message you're giving your church is out of balance. Yours is a grace-filled church that talks deeply of the love of Jesus Christ. But that's all you talk about. Rarely will you discuss sin and separation. Do you even believe that sin separates us from the love of God? There are distinct rights and wrongs. I believe that God gives us these distinct ideas of right and wrong to keep us safe. You're not setting those boundaries for others in your church. By not speaking about sin you're creating immature followers of Jesus. This church is spiritual milk for us, not meat.

We sat and listened intently to our friends. They are gracious and wise. The week after I took on the job of starting a church in Brooklyn, my friend met me at the Alehouse. He sat down, bought me a beer, and asked, "Are you going to be okay? How're you feeling about the new job?"

"I think I made a mistake." My friend gave me the space to say that. I just needed the space to feel in over my head and unqualified. I needed the space to doubt that I could lead a new church. My friend gave me that space. Conversations with my friend were like that. I continue to credit encouragement and mentorship from this particular friend as a reason that I continue in ministry. But in his mind I'd become untethered from the gospel message. I'd forgotten about the sin and separation aspect of the cross.

The other couple reiterated my friend's sentiment: "Your preaching is like a tire with too much air. There's a bubble that keeps the church out of balance." The couple was leaving our church. They wanted to find a place that gave their children better boundaries in which to live. No one touched the salami plate.

Our friends were there to guide me through the ins and outs of ministry. Our friends were there to help me raise money, create timelines, deal with difficult people, and simply pray. Our friends and mentors were there to counsel us through the difficult personal issues that arise during marriage. They were there to challenge our church in its diversity, or lack thereof. In short, our friends and mentors were directly tied to each and every one of our celebrations, every one of our failures, our joy, our pain, our lives; and they weren't coming back to support us any longer.

My dad was my friend's mentor, and when my father transitioned, the pain of saying good-bye was as profound for him as it was for me. My friend credited my father with his professional growth and maturity. He cited my father's gracious conversations as the model for healthy relationships within an organization. Outside of his own father, my father had the greatest influence in his life. My friend still mourned the loss of my dad.

They were right. I didn't preach on sin. I didn't talk about how our sin separates us from God. I didn't see strong spiritual growth in our community. If my friends and mentors wanted a pastor who spoke clearly on sin, separation, and an acceptance of Jesus Christ, then I wasn't that pastor. If they wanted a church that spoke about our sin and need for forgiveness, we were not that church.

My friends and mentors were right about the fact that I no longer believed in sin and separation. I spent much of my time quietly doubting an issue that many believe to be a central tenet of Christianity. My father had defined sin for me in my growing up; by that definition, she would be sent to a fiery hell. My father was in violation of the laws of sin he passed along, and while our ideas and theology evolve over the years, it's often the values passed down from our ancestors that have a stronghold deep within our DNA.

I was in the unique position of denying my father's early concepts of sin, and, at the same time, cultivating a new theology of sin that accepted my father as beloved. I worked out my dogmas and ideologies on stage in front of a church community, and, yes, those ideas were often out of balance in the attempt to affirm my father's transition and navigate all I'd been raised to believe.

The Matthew 18 delegation led by my friend and his wife were correct in their assessment of our church and my teaching. I could confirm that one loses a sense of balance when one's pastor father—who defines all of one's spiritual life for thirty-plus years—soon transitions to the female gender, and obliterates one's whole theological framework in the process. Not only will that create an out-of-balance theology of sin that manifests in Sunday morning sermons, but it also drives one to drink.

My friend's personal separation from our church freed me to make the divorce complete. To his credit, my friend continued to mentor me from afar and check in on my mental health. I discussed openly with him my struggles and doubts surrounding our church's move to inclusion. My friend, firmly entrenched on the other side, continued to offer up himself as mentor, making space for me to process what exactly a new affirming theology could look like in our church community. He knew that an official separation between the Harvest Network and Forefront was imminent, and L believe that we walked each other through the process.

－〜－

Many years before, my grandparents had sat with my father at the dining room table. I was thirteen, and rarely sat down to breakfast; I was anxious that I would miss the bus. As I sat with my grandparents and father at the table, my Pop finally asked my father the question that we were all there to witness: "Will you take over this organization and ministry from us?" I looked at my father across the table and found myself deeply saddened by his face.

My father replied, "I'll accept the job to run this organization. Thank you for your offer."

Yet my father's face said something different. It said, "I will take this job so that I can support my family. I'll run this organization because it's familiar, and I'm comfortable in it. I'll accept this position and, in the process, lose a piece of my soul." We hugged and breakfast was over. I made it on time to the bus.

The Harvest Network of now was not my father's organization, much as it wasn't his when he accepted the position in 1989.

My friend and I met at Franklin Park, and I told him that we were making the official move toward full inclusion. He invited me on one last pastors' retreat. He gave us a chance to celebrate all that had been. He allowed Jubi and me to say good-bye on our own terms, and he confirmed that there would always be a friendship between us, regardless of the fact that we were on different journeys. We had one more retreat with Bert, Derrick, Scott, and the rest of the Harvest pastors. We had a chance to say good-bye. A few weeks later, we were off the official Harvest Network roster of churches.

The other well-intentioned pastors outside of the Harvest Network needed to know that our church was now inclusive. They had done their best to support my family in the pain of my father's transition. They had prayed an impassioned prayer for my father and for my family: "Lord, I pray that Paul might finally realize that this is not how you made him, and he would turn away from his false self."

I called, and, as always, they were gracious. The well-intentioned are always gracious. I sincerely thanked them for their financial support and then told them that they wouldn't get the return on investment that they were looking for. Our church's metrics were no longer centered on attendance and baptisms but rather on the ways in which we love the marginalized, specifically the LGBTQIA community. I apologized that our metrics were changing. My well-intentioned pastor friend let me know that they were praying for good things for our church but that our official partnership was over. We were written off as a net loss. Our investors would support newer churches that led baptism revivals. Our investors would fly out to pray for those pastors. Our time ended.

My ninety-plus-year-old grandparents still send us a check each month. They're both very concerned that the cost of living in New York City might end our family's time there and our ministry. It's sweet and loving, and I'm grateful. While my grandfather is getting too old for church ministry, he did work to help me secure extra funding from the church he attended. He leveraged his position on the church missions team to get our church a substantial amount of money when the church was getting started, for which I'm incredibly thankful.

My father's transition sent my grandparents into a state of confusion. They didn't have much experience with transgender people, and they weren't exactly sure why their son would want to dress up as a woman. My father set some boundaries around her parents and chose not to see them, more to protect them than her. I flew out to try and explain to them what it meant to be transgender, and what my father's experience looked like. My grandparents nodded along and asked few questions. Their body language betrayed the fact that they were content to view their son as an anomaly that they would never quite understand, or even see again.

When I leaned over to hug my grandmother good-bye, she held me tight and whispered, "You promise me you don't become a girl like your father."

"No, Grandma!"

I recognized that my protest was futile.

"Okay, Grandma. I promise not to become a woman like Dad."

It was under these circumstances that I told the leader of the missions team at my Grandpa's church that we were questioning our stance on inclusivity for the queer community. We were grateful for their help and prayers, but we wanted to end our partnership with the church. She asked a few questions as to whether or not our decision was related to my father. I told her it was, and there was a longer pause. With her charming southern accent, the leader of the missions team relayed her final thoughts: "Okay, Jonathan. Thanks for letting us know. We're no longer going to financially support the work you're doing, but we appreciate you. And Jonathan, I'm not going to tell your grandfather about this. I'm not sure he'd be able to take it."

Chapter 10

A JUST AND GENEROUS CHURCH

When people think of church inclusion, they immediately go to the "clobber" passages. There are seven passages in the Bible that are commonly read as prohibiting same-sex intercourse. These are the passages used to justify exclusion of the LGBTQIA community from the kingdom of God. When studied in context, they can also be used as justification for same-sex relationships and full inclusion in the kingdom of God.

Our church took a different approach.

When it comes to biblical hermeneutics and inclusivity, our church skipped over Scripture's famous clobber passages. There is much more in our Scriptures that speaks to inclusion without describing the physical act of sex. And what about my dad? The passages in Scripture that call gender fluidity a sin are even more rare. In fact, from what I gather, there's only one passage that speaks in the realm of being transgender: "A woman shall not wear a man's apparel, nor shall a man put on a woman's garment; for whoever does such things is abhorrent to the Lord your God" (Deut. 22:5).

We can go a number of ways with this text. First, even among Jewish rabbis, there is no agreement as to what this verse means precisely. A general agreement among scholars is that this passage does *not* refer to transgender people who wear clothing more aligned with their gender identity.[1]

Is it possible that this text referred to marriage and adultery? The following chapter speaks of marriage violations, and we know that it was custom for genders to remain separate until marriage. Was this an admonition not to deceive through use of clothing? Did this passage speak about hiding male soldiers who didn't want to leave for war, and to women soldiers made to take up armor and sword and fight? All are plausible readings.

As a church, we wanted to convey that healing and restoration come from the freedom to live out one's true identity. To take that identity and dissect it through Old Testament proof texting seemed to miss the point entirely. While we're debating the meanings of ancient texts, so many in the queer community are presently marginalized, hurt, and even dying for attempting to live out the truth of how they are perfectly created in the image of God.

I think there is incredible writing around meanings of ancient texts with regard to queer theology (Colby Martin's *Unclobber* and Matthew Vines's *God and the Gay Christian* come to mind).[2] But instead, our church leadership studied the Scripture and worked diligently to highlight stories of God's love for humanity rather than dissecting language and words. Taking a cue from Rob Bell's *What Is the Bible?*[3] we told the stories in our church, and we wrestled under the auspices of *unity* in Christ, and not *uniformity*. One of these stories is that of Abraham being told to sacrifice his son Isaac:

> After these things God tested Abraham. He said to him, "Abraham!" And he said, "Here I am." He said, "Take your son, your only son Isaac, whom you love,

and go to the land of Moriah, and offer him there as a burnt offering on one of the mountains that I shall show you." (Gen. 22:1–2)

Why is this significant? Abraham was incredibly old when Sarah had Isaac. God said he would build a mighty nation from Abraham, and then God tells him to sacrifice his son? This seems despicable. This seems like God is angry and vengeful and full of malice. I don't want to worship a God that asks someone to sacrifice his or her child. As a parent, I especially feel this way. I don't know if I can hang with this messed-up God.

We have to remember that we're reading stories of people who lived in different stages of consciousness, with very different ways of seeing and understanding the world. We too relate to the world through our place in time, and our worldviews are shaped accordingly. We might remember what life looked like in generations past, but we struggle to comprehend what life was really like then. It's hard for us to read our Scriptures, especially the stories of Genesis, and remember that we're reading about a group of people living in an age when killing was an everyday part of life. So, when we're reading early texts, we have to read with the eyes of those living at the time. We have to read with the eyes of people doing their best to hear God in a new way and live life in the way that God might intend.

There is a fair amount of evidence that during the Bronze Age, when Abraham's story takes place, ancient Near East cultures sacrificed children. We have archaeological descriptions of Ammonites sacrificing children. We have descriptions of sacrifices to the god Molech. We find out that child sacrifice is relatively common in the ancient Near East, done to ensure that crops will be plentiful and wars will be won. This may seem barbaric to us now, but we have to put ourselves in the place of people who lived in the tribal age. So it wouldn't be out of the ordinary for an Israelite to think that God would ask for a child sacrifice:

> When they came to the place that God had shown him, Abraham built an altar there and laid the wood in order. He bound his son Isaac, and laid him on the altar, on top of the wood. Then Abraham reached out his hand and took the knife to kill his son. But the angel of the Lord called to him from heaven, and said, "Abraham, Abraham!" And he said, "Here I am." He said, "Do not lay your hand on the boy or do anything to him; for now I know that you fear God, since you have not withheld your son, your only son, from me." (Gen. 22:9–12)

If I place myself for a moment in the consciousness of the Bronze Age, I'm immediately uncomfortable with the command my God gives me *not* to kill my son. As I said, child sacrifice is common. Gods command it. Each nation believes that child sacrifice helps win wars and bring about good crops. And now the Hebrew God is saying that there is no need to sacrifice children. This is an absolutely radical idea!

In fact, people had such a hard time with this idea—that God could be so "radically loving" as to not want children sacrificed—that God has to command it again in the book of Leviticus: "You shall not give any of your offspring to sacrifice them to Molech, and so profane the name of your God: I am the LORD" (Lev. 18:21).

The story of Abraham and Isaac began the expanding of my theological imagination. Is it possible that our

Scriptures are showing us that there is a loving God, and that God is working within our worldview and consciousness to bring pure love and peace, to bring shalom? Is it possible that we are so loved by God that a loving God stoops down to our level to show us these little glimpses of what God's love really looks like? For a tribal nation, God's love meant that God's children didn't need to be sacrificed to bring God joy. There was already joy. There's a gracious God working within our consciousness to show us that God is far more gracious and loving than we can imagine. God will make us uncomfortable in our time and place in order to push us toward the possibility that something far greater, more inclusive, and more loving is possible.

Surprising as it may sound, a story in our Scriptures about the rape of women created in me the theological framework for becoming an inclusive church.

> When you go to war against your enemies and the LORD your God delivers them into your hands and you take captives, suppose you see among the captives a beautiful woman whom you desire and want to marry, and so you bring her home to your house: she shall her shave her head, pare her nails, discard her captive's garb, and shall remain in your house a full month, mourning for her father and mother; after that you may go in to her and be her husband, and she shall be your wife. If you are not satisfied with her, you shall let her go free and not sell her for money. You must not treat her as a slave, since you have dishonored her. (Deut. 21:10–14)

Let's start out by saying that this should bother us. This is pretty terrible. Regardless of anything else, it's sad that humanity treated and still treats women this way. But again, I look at the consciousness of the ancient Near East.

In some Bibles, this is called the "spoils of war" passage, and for a reason. Again, we're in a place of tribal consciousness, which means that other tribes were seen as a threat. They were a threat to one's land, to one's ethnicity, and to one's entire being. When people went into battle in the Iron Age culture, they made sure that everything was wiped out. That would ensure that there was no way for a tribe to infiltrate or mix with another tribe at all. It was common in the rules of war to completely destroy towns. An army would completely destroy each person in that town.

Soldiers would completely destroy livestock. Children might be taken as sex slaves. It was not uncommon for a soldier to rape a woman of another tribe before she was killed.

Keeping in mind that I'm reading stories from another age and time, I worked to read the text with different eyes. If you see a beautiful woman when you are sacking another tribe, take her home and make her your wife.

Remember, this is hard to digest, but we have to put ourselves in their consciousness. What does God command here? Women were property to be raped and killed, and now I have to wait a month and then make her my wife? The command to delay was as radical as having to marry.

Have her shave her head and trim her nails. These are Hebrew signs of mourning, which is a very real part of humanity. So instead of treating a woman like an object, raping and killing her, you are now commanded to allow her to mourn, which shows her humanity.

After thirty days, you can make her your wife; but if you don't like her, then you must not dishonor her or sell her as a slave. A woman was property. But if you don't like a captive woman, you must give her a certificate of divorce.

This is a big deal. Normally, a woman who lived and had no husband was sold into slavery and made a prostitute. The command in this situation is that she be given a certificate of divorce, which grants her status and ensures that she most likely will not face prostitution.

Can we see for one second how radical this passage is? Is it possible that there were soldiers who didn't want to follow this law? "You mean I have to feed, clothe, and house this person? She's property!" "You're telling me that I can't kill this person? God, what if she reproduces with someone else, and their tribe comes back stronger than ever?" Can you imagine what other nations might think? "Wow, we allowed some of them to live. We're getting soft."

Is it possible that people didn't want to follow this controversial commandment? Is it possible that followers of God were split over this, thinking that their God would never allow non-chosen people to live?

Once again, I ask myself the same questions. Is it possible that God exists, that the Bible exists, along a continuum of human growth and consciousness? Is it possible that God is working toward a perfect and loving peace, and that God is doing it one small step at a time? Is it possible that our Scriptures are showing us a loving God, and that God is working within our worldview and consciousness to bring pure love and peace, to bring shalom?

The beauty of this God is brought to light once again through the lens of Jesus. We get to see a loving God working to guide God's people toward greater inclusion. It's evident in Jesus' first sermon, in which he quotes from the scroll of Isaiah:

> The spirit of the Lord GOD is upon me,
>   because the LORD has anointed me;
> he has sent me to bring good news to the oppressed,
>   to bind up the brokenhearted,
> to proclaim liberty to the captives
>   and release to the prisoners;
> to proclaim the year of the LORD's favor,
>   and the day of vengeance of our God.
>
> Isa. 61:1–2

I read about a revolt against Roman occupation in a city called Sepphoris, right around the time that Jesus was born. The city was about four miles outside of Jesus' hometown of Nazareth. As a result of the revolt, it was reported that the Roman General Varus burned the city to the ground. About three thousand Galileans were either killed or sold into slavery by the Romans, and about two thousand Galileans were crucified in a single day.

Imagine what it would be like to witness such a catastrophe if you were an inhabitant of Nazareth at that time. Imagine the fear, the anger, and the sadness. What would victims desire for the Romans, or any of the other non-Jewish oppressors throughout your people's long history of suffering? Where would you find hope?

And what does Jesus do? In his first sermon back in Nazareth, he brings back the Scripture of Isaiah. He walks into the synagogue, he unrolls the scroll, and he says these words:

> The Spirit of the Lord is upon me
>   because he has anointed me
>   to bring good news to the poor.
> He has sent me to proclaim release to the captives

and recovery of sight to the blind,
   to let the oppressed go free,
to proclaim the year of the Lord's favor.
                                    Luke 4:18–19

But Jesus leaves out one crucial, life-changing line. Jesus does not say, "And the day of vengeance of our God." He rolls up the scroll, returns it, sits down, and says, "Today this scripture has been fulfilled in your hearing" (v. 21).

People are amazed at Jesus' teaching, but Jesus realizes that he has not made them uncomfortable enough. He reminds them of the time that God protected their enemies in Sidon. Then he reminds them of a time that Israel was afflicted with a skin disease, but only a king from Syria was healed. In a few simple lines, Jesus tells the people in his hometown that the justice of God doesn't happen through revenge fantasies. The love of God is not shown through strength or by might. The affirmation of God's love is given to Israelites *and* their enemies.

Once Jesus explains this to the people, they want to kill him! They want revenge! They want God's vengeance! Once again, God moves God's people into unfamiliar territory where they're confronted with the notion that God is more loving and more inclusive than they ever imagined.

―――

There are countless other stories in Scripture that, while they might seem odd to our modern consciousness, demonstrate God's love for all the different people of the world.

For example, Peter dreams of a sheet falling from heaven with all sorts of unkosher foods on it, signifying to

Peter that he can now eat the same food as the Gentiles. The vision itself provokes a crisis in Peter: "Surely not Lord! I've followed the laws, and my ancestors before followed the laws." The Spirit of the Lord tells Peter not to call unclean what God has made clean. God pushes Peter into an uncomfortable place where he must acknowledge that God's acceptance of all people extends beyond Peter's perspective of God (see Acts 10).

Let me ask you some questions:

What if you told me that you were going to start running? What if you said, "Jonathan, I've never run before, but I'm going to start." And I said, "Great! There is a marathon tomorrow, and I've signed you up." What would you say to me? "Jonathan, I just started running today! There's no way I can run a marathon tomorrow! That's stupid!" And what if I got really mad and was like, "Come on! What's your problem? Do it now!"

That would be ridiculous for me to do, because change takes awhile. In humanity, a change of consciousness takes awhile.

What if you stood up and announced, "I'm going to start studying chemistry." And I said, "Great! I have this deadline with the pharmaceutical company, and I need you to create a new drug to fight diphtheria, and I need it by tomorrow." You'd say, "I just started studying chemistry! I don't even know all of the periodic elements yet!"

That would be equally ridiculous. We're never asked to completely grasp a concept overnight. We're not asked to take impossible steps before God. Rather, consciousness comes step by step, little by little, with lots of growing pains and new ideas. It comes with changing brain chemistry and new neural pathways and lots of prayer. It comes through conversation, and, slowly but surely, expanding our ideas about how absolutely big and infinite our God truly is. It comes with a sibling who announces that she or he is gay, and with a father who transitions to another gender. It comes through invoking curiosity and the questions that arise when we sit next to the Muslim person on a subway, or interact with the life story of someone we've always considered an outsider.

The fact that we're even bothered by these stories shows that we have moved forward. We have expanded our consciousness. The fact that I struggle with these stories in Scripture shows that, over thousands of years and many ages, we've moved an incredible distance toward the infinite confirmation, acknowledgment, and beauty of all humanity.

So maybe, just maybe, the fact that God moves us to bigger consciousness slowly, in steps, instead of asking the impossible of us, shows just how loving this God is. Maybe the fact that God moves us step by step is God showing us the utmost patience. Maybe it's God showing us the utmost grace. Maybe it's God showing us the utmost love. Perhaps it's God moving us toward the radical love and inclusivity that God so desires. And maybe we're moving along the same spectrum in regard to gender identity.

Citing the passages mentioned here, and more, we continually asked our church community to imagine the possibility for us to be a part of God's story. In his book *Disarming Scripture*, Derrick Flood writes, "The correct interpretation of scripture always comes down to how we love. The Bible was never intended to be our master, placing a burden on our back. It was intended to act like a servant, leading us to love God, others, and ourselves."[4]

Is Scripture a living and breathing work, or is it dead? If Scripture is dead, then our church's reasoning for inclusivity is dead with it. If our Scripture is still alive, and if

God is still writing God's story, then is it possible that God has called us to play a part in reflecting the uncomfortable and radical inclusion we see throughout the Scriptures?

Is it possible that Scripture is talking about reflecting God's intention for inclusivity in us when Jesus tells his disciples, "Very truly I tell you, whoever believes in me will also do the works that I do, and, in fact, will do greater works than these" (John 14:12)? Are we able to do those greater things?

Jesus and Peter both break with the tradition of Scripture because they're compelled by the Spirit to welcome the "other" as a full member in the kingdom of God. How might the Spirit be leading our church to do the same?

We asked our church to imagine Christianity two thousand years from now. What would those Christians say about us? Would they find it appalling that we discriminated against the LGBTQIA community, in much the same way that we find the "spoils of war" passage appalling now?

Would they see the popular American Evangelical stance—to be welcoming but not affirming—an affront to the decency of all humanity, and barbaric at best?

How would that future church see us, if we continue to resist the calling of Scripture's arc? How do we look to the future church when we marginalize those who are right here in our church?

~

"D" is a member and leader at our church who identifies as asexual:

> When you "come out" as asexual and aromantic, it
> tends to be a non-issue with most people. At worst,

people are confused, skeptical, or dismissive. I had self-identified as asexual for several years, but hadn't felt the need to disclose this to others. Being asexual in a world of allosexual (our term for non-asexual) people can be terribly isolating.[5]

When I first talked to D about their (D's pronouns are they/them/their) sexual identity, I once again found myself feeling in the dark for the correct answers. My unfamiliarity with what it means to be asexual felt embarrassing at best.

I believed D's story to be pivotal in the way our church embraces one's story and promotes infinite and unimaginable belonging.

We prayed that D's wrestling with their identity could be done in the safety and love of our church community. Regardless of knowing very little of what it meant to be asexual, our continued teaching surrounding the arc of God's commitment toward love, inclusion, and belonging begged us to support D first, and then walk with them in creating clarity around their identity.

> [My identity] is a part of me that is affirmed and celebrated. With each new shift in identity, my Forefront family has taken it in stride. When I switched pronouns and began using they/them/theirs, I was surprised that people were excited for me. Having agonized for months, I had forgotten that this decision called for rejoicing. It's been confusing, frustrating, heartbreaking, and anxiety inducing. It has also been exciting and empowering and cause for celebration. And in each of those moments, I know that I need not walk alone.[6]

These are the stories and the questions that allow us to bring our inquisitive minds through the doors of the church. Is God's word still alive? If so, how do we play a part in God's story of infinite love and inclusion? D's story highlights our commitment as a church to walk in the arc of God's never-ending push toward inclusion and grace.

Unfortunately, moving forward with a new biblical hermeneutic requires courage that few churches possess. We're seeing the effects in churches that are afraid that walking toward inclusion is an offense to God.

Diana Butler Bass speaks of a misguided view of Scripture that often keeps the church from moving toward inclusion of people like D—our vertical and hierarchal understanding of God. As Christians, we've spent way too much time with a vertical reading of our Bibles. What does Butler Bass mean by "vertical" constructions of God?[7]

We hang heaven at the top of our vertical construction. That's where God resides, and it's the place we attain—heaven. We're on earth, a place often seen as broken and getting worse. For those who don't measure up to the standards of God, we have a third tier—hell—which lies beneath our "broken" earth and is punishment for not looking upward.

The vertical construction of Christianity invades our sensibilities until it becomes second nature to believe that there is another place above for which we strive—and one below, which we avoid at all costs. And what are the costs of avoiding the tier below us?

In a vertical construction of God, we ask what it is we have to believe. How do we believe? How do I gain membership in the ascension to a better place?

Based on those questions, we get to work interpreting a rather flat and literal reading of Scripture. We line up beliefs and opinions designed to measure the worthiness of one who will ascend or descend, depending on their perspective. Finally, we create a meritocracy, designed to make our vertical construction exclusive. Our membership in another place is gained through creating complete clarity and structure around the first two questions: "Am I reading Scripture in such a way that it's acceptable to the gatekeepers of heaven (whoever they may be)? Can I put a check next to each moral platitude and practice that keeps me out of the danger of hell? If that's the case then I'm able to join the membership of heaven."[8]

The tragedy of the vertical construction of God and the Scriptures is that relationships are no longer essential to the Christian ethic. Regardless of the fact that our Christian faith is centered on the mutually loving relationship of the triune God, we throw out the Trinity for the sake of the letter, the law, and our membership in another place. There's no need for relational investment.

There was no surprise at my father being let go from her position in her church-planting organization. She threatened the very existence of Christianity's vertical construct. To accept my father meant going against a flat reading of Scripture. It meant that one less box could be checked on their list of moral platitudes. Worse yet, acceptance of my father and others like her threatened the membership of Christians far more concerned with getting it right and moving upward than establishing and upholding loving relationships.

As long as Christianity continues to espouse a vertically constructed theology that leaves God's creation outside of relationship, it will surely lose people quickly. This line of thinking almost ended Grace's relationship to God.

Grace was heavily involved in a sports-focused Christian ministry at her college. Having received her faith from her Palestinian grandmother, Grace thought this ministry to be a natural extension of her Christ-centered life.

Through her college years, Grace came to a place where she was comfortable in her growing personal notion that she was, indeed, queer.

"I came to terms with it really quickly; it's weirdly something that comforts me. I knew that nothing about me was changed or different. It made sense. I loved and liked people for who they were, not what they looked like or what gender they were. It just fit."[9]

It was time for Grace to talk with her mentors in the organization. She wanted to be forthright about coming out:

> When I told [my ministry leader] it was a different story. I was supposed to be working for the ministry the following year, getting paid by them. So, I go to coffee and tell her that I'm into this woman. And she responds with some statistic stating that most gay people have "darkness in their pasts."
>
> It was like a knife to the heart. Her words were judgmental, hurtful, shaming, and frustrating. Immediately, she broke my trust. I don't have f*ck*ng DARKNESS in my past. A week later, she took me out to lunch and apologized for her response. She said she should have thought more about it before responding. But also said that the organization does not believe that being gay is okay, and if I wanted to work for them the following year, I would have to "not live that lifestyle."

Grace didn't lose faith in God. Her relationship with the beliefs of others greatly affected her faith in God. Her loss of Christianity was an outcome of the larger belief in the vertical structure of Christianity that simply disregards humanity in order to align with "right thinking."

Grace talked about how her belief in church and religion waned as pastors spoke on sexual sin and the submission of women, once again forsaking relationship for their idea of sound doctrine. Grace has another word for all of the "right thinking" and "sound doctrines." She calls them "weapons." The weapons used on Grace were damaging, and stopped her from believing that she was whole:

> I had spent so much time working to reconcile the distinctions between what Christians said about gay people and what I knew God actually felt. I know my God. He loves me. I didn't change when I came out. I was not different. I didn't treat people worse or better. My intelligence did not change—I was, in fact, more open and capable of growth, learning, questioning, and loving. Why would me dating a woman change how God loved me? Christians have been failing the queer community for generations. They have worked hard to keep God from us, when, in fact, God is needed so very much.

No wonder people leave churches in droves. Ultimately, it was the love of those around her that brought Grace back to a loving God.

> With a couple other queer friends we decided to do a little gathering to welcome in some other queer Christians. And it was like I hadn't even remembered what it was like to be my full self around people. I didn't know them all yet, but we connected in a way that only people with a shared experience can connect.

We had all been through different things, and had
different church experiences, but it was amazing to
be queer and talk about God. To joke about church,
and talk about our experiences dating other women.
Just that tiny bit of connection, that ability to be yourself, it's a f*ck*ng revolution.

Relationships are fast becoming the new currency in
our global culture. As we develop new relationships that
span cultures, tribes, lifestyles, and orientations, we're
quickly recognizing that there is less need for platitudes and
the exclusivity of a heaven. It's possible that God's kingdom is here among us. Yes, that feels revolutionary.

More than ever before, we're recognizing that God
isn't *upstairs* somewhere, but rather in and among us.

In order for Christianity to proclaim the good news,
we need to stop asking the questions of the vertically constructed theology, and instead ask, "To whom does humanity belong?" The answer is profoundly simple. We belong
to the infinitely loving and gracious Creator who shows us
that God has been with us all along. D belongs to an infinite
and loving Creator. Grace belongs to an infinite and loving
Creator. So do I. So does my dad.

━━

As a church, it was our job to shine the light on our identity
in God. When our church members told us that they no
longer believed in God, I could tell them with the utmost
sincerity that I didn't believe in *that* God either. I didn't
believe in the vertically constructed universe. I didn't
believe in forsaking our one, wild life here for whatever was
above or below. I told our church members that I wasn't

sure I could even give words to what my expression of God looked like. I gave them permission to feel the same way. I told them that we could travel together toward the God that Paul Tillich famously says "doesn't exist, but rather is the ground of all existence."

Our church is working to reclaim God through celebrating the mystery that we believe the infinite and unimaginable comes down as God Incarnate and lives among us. God Incarnate shows us the fullness of deep and lasting relationships with deeply flawed humanity to the point that God Incarnate is willing to suffer and die with us. We celebrate the mystery that our God Incarnate continues to live in relationship with us as Spirit.

Our church can reclaim the wonder and imagination of Christianity by continually asking the question, "To whom do we belong?" Together we travel with this question, making meaning along the way.

Paula Responds

After I transitioned, I took time off from the church. I went to a couple of mainline Protestant churches, but the liturgy did not hold much meaning for me. I was not welcome in the Evangelical churches where I would enjoy the worship, so I just stopped going to church. It was an important time of healing.

Eighteen months later—on Father's Day 2015—I returned to the church when I attended my first service at Highlands Church in Denver. When the music began, the tears began to flow as they had not flowed since that night, years before, when I knew I had been called to authenticity. I sobbed throughout the service. When my friend and fellow pastor Jen brought me Communion, cupped in her hands, I knew I was home. I had found a community into which I could bring all of me. It was a community that believed in original blessing, not original sin. It was a community that believed God loves us just as we are, no strings attached, no changes required. On the strength of the teachings of Jesus as expressed in a local body of believers, my faith returned. I was nurtured and fed at Highlands. I found healing and hope. And in my spiritual life, I began to thrive—for several reasons.

First and foremost, I am in the right gender, the one intended for me. My life is difficult, to be sure, but internally I am at far greater peace.

Second, I had never realized how difficult it is to hold positions that, in your heart, do not square with common sense. It has always been obvious to me that LGBTQ people, Roman Catholics, Jews, and Buddhists were not the enemy; nor were they under the influence of any enemy. That is not to say evil does not exist, but evil is not tied to a particular religion or people group.

Third, my faith grows because my hermeneutic has changed. When I was young, I accepted the typical Evangelical hermeneutic. When I came to question the Evangelical stance on homosexual relationships, I argued from my hermeneutic that what the apostle Paul was writing about was not what gay relationships are today.

But even with an Evangelical hermeneutic, it was a stretch to find anything wrong with being transgender. The Bible was silent on the subject; though, since Evangelicals lost the culture wars on marriage equality, they suddenly "discovered" new understandings of Scripture on issues of gender identity. Their new understandings are wrong. To say Genesis teaches that God created people only male or female is to ignore the plethora of intersex conditions that exist in the world. To say they are a result of some kind of original sin is to strain credulity on the commonsense meter.

My hermeneutic shifted because the inconsistencies inherent in the Evangelical hermeneutic were too much to bear.

Today's U.S. Supreme Court is evenly divided between "originalists" and "non-originalists." The "originalists" believe the Constitution should be interpreted strictly according to the understanding of its adopters at the time it was written. The "non-originalists" believe it is a living, breathing document that will change as our understanding changes. A lot has changed in 250 years. To consider normative the understandings of one group of white males at one specific period in time is to do a disservice to the founding fathers and to the men and women who lead our nation today. We have grown in our knowledge and understanding. Reinterpretations are necessary in light of that growth.

The same is true of Scripture. And the truth is that the church has acknowledged this for centuries. Galileo was placed under house arrest by the church because he believed the earth revolved around the sun. The church abandoned that view centuries ago for a simple reason; it was wrong. The church has adjusted its position on slavery, divorce and remarriage, transracial marriage, and other cultural issues. If history is any indicator—and it is—it will also adjust its position on LGBTQ acceptance. The only question is how long it will take.

The church moved on each of these subjects when they realized their previous position was no longer tenable. The sun does not revolve around the earth. Slavery is never alright. On these subjects and others, the church has always operated from a "non-originalist" perspective. It makes adjustments when scientific discovery demands it.

As Derek Flood suggests in his book *Disarming Scripture*, there is a trajectory to Scripture, one that flows from a punitive God to a gracious God. There have always been unquestioning followers and faithful questioners among the followers of God. Both groups are evident from one end of Scripture to the other. But when quoting from the Hebrew Scriptures, Jesus quoted the faithful questioners, not the unquestioning faithful. He also took liberties with the text, often restating it, "You have heard it said, but I say. . . ."

All these understandings freed my faith in every bit as profound a way as my female body freed me from the male body that felt so foreign. They gave me hope, and life, and faith.

As my faith thrived, I began to wonder just how many others were in the same circumstances. I am not speaking of those who are transgender, but of those whose faith has become dormant under the weight of the suspension of disbelief. If a renewed faith could come through both of my transitions, my gender transition and my faith transition, how many others are having similar experiences, looking for a church like Highlands, or the congregation I serve as a pastor, Left Hand Church?

Based on the experience of Highlands, Left Hand, Denver Community Church, Forefront Church in Brooklyn, and a plethora of others, there are a lot of humans ready to embrace a Christianity focused more on right action than right belief, on God as the ultimate suffering participant instead of God as the ultimate threatener, and a church organizing for the common good instead of a church focused on its own self-preservation.

As I move forward, I am more hopeful about the church than I have ever been, more at peace with my Creator than I have ever been, and more vibrantly alive than I ever thought possible.

For the first time in my life, I have hope that the words of Pierre Teilhard de Chardin will come true:

> The day will come when, after harnessing the ether, the winds, the tides, gravitation, we shall harness for God the energies of love. And, on that day, for the second time in the history of the world, man will have discovered fire.[10]

Chapter 11

TOV

"You have got to be so happy for your father!" Paula's friend hugged me and asked my permission to share in the genuine excitement of my father's new life.

"I am happy for my father!" I was able to reply. "I'm happy that she found this church and each of you. It makes a big difference in my life."

My father and I attended a progressive Christian conference together. Paula recently took membership with Highlands Church where she lived in Denver, Colorado, and attended the conference with their staff and leadership. The church gave her voice to speak, something she sorely missed after her coming out.

Paul spent much of his professional time speaking at some of the largest Christian Evangelical churches in America. His speaking ability brought him through the ranks from young preacher to national conference speaker. Paul was at his best on stage, where he had a gentle charisma that deeply resonated with his listeners.

Paula's transition forcibly suspended her speaking career. The gift that brought Paul to national prominence and supported his family was temporarily silenced in Paula. Highlands Church gave her that voice again, in the process returning Paula's sense of professional calling.

The church gave her the opportunity to share her thirty-plus years of expertise in church health and church growth. The church brought with it a community that embraced Paula and confirmed what she'd already started to believe, that her membership was simply the fact that she belonged to God and was made perfectly in God's image. The church ushered in personal justice for Paula. The justice of God is always restorative, and it was no different at Highlands.

I watched from afar and celebrated as the community at Highlands, little by little, restored the parts of my father that were the casualties of her transition. Paula was here at the conference with the fully restored gifts that had been temporarily left behind with Paul. This was her element. We hugged, and my father introduced me to each of her friends.

Now it's true that Paul had friends. Paul's friends spoke at the same conferences, invested together, and made dinner plans in convention center hallways. If Paul wasn't with his friends, then he talked shop with his important acquaintances, and gave genuine time and response to those who stopped to give their thanks or to seek out advice.

Paul had friends; Paula had been lonely. Paula no longer made dinner plans with other influential pastors. Upon her transition, Paula became the "shop talk" at the national conferences. About two years after my father's transition, I received a rash of texts within hours, all saying the same thing: "Tell me that what they're saying about your dad isn't true." It dawned on me that the big church-planting conference had kicked off, and Paula was indeed the topic around the convention center. "It's true," I replied.

Our church had just gone through the inclusion process, and although we weren't explicitly disinvited, no one in the conference went out of their way to encourage our attendance. I fell out of the membership of the well-intentioned and headed down a slippery slope toward whatever was below. It was lonely; I was lonely. I can't imagine Paula's loneliness.

Paul had the luxury of being defined by what he did and what he had. What he did gave him a platform, and in the Evangelical church world, he had abundance. The transition took that from her.

So, at the progressive church conference, my father went around the group, introducing each of her new friends; with each smile, gesture, and pat on the back came an overwhelming sense of relief that her gifts were restored and her loneliness abated.

That's what I said; here's what I thought: I need my parent. I need my dad. The prospect of losing my dad and carrying the responsibility to care for my dad was more than I could bear, and you saved me from that reckoning. You saved me from the constant worry that my father might be a victim. The church she loved so dearly disowned her, as they do so many others who identify as transgender. I carried with me the genuine fear that my father might become one of the 41 percent who could no longer carry the weight of rejection and attempt to end their lives.

"Yes, I'm definitely happy for her."

My father's friend took on a new face, one that offered vulnerability and safety. This face was different from faces of the well-intentioned. There was an authenticity to her face and a need for me to know that, as with my father, genuine relationship was offered to all at their church. Her face was an invitation: "Are you happy that your father gets to live out her true identity?" Her tone matched her face, and my father's friend wanted sincerity.

My father is living out her true identity. She is out-wardly the woman whom she had always been, just out of our periphery. For my father, that is freedom, and that makes me happy.

On a subsequent visit to our home, I watched my father's movements—simple—a walk to the kitchen and then back to the table. I noticed that she picked up her com-puter and walked to the oversized leather chair. I watched as she answered email. Each of her movements looked easy and untroubled. I worked to remember a time when Paul evoked a similar peace in his being. I thought back to our childhood and recognized that the memories of Paul at peace in his physical being were rather significant because they were few and far between. Paula was at home in her being. For that I was happy. She no longer carried a body for which she had limited use.

I was proud of her transition. I was proud of the fact that her waking up to greet life was a courageous act known only by a few. That made me happy for my father.

My father's advocacy work made me happy. She vol-unteered with the local PFLAG chapter in her area, and, with her understated and gracious charisma, spoke plainly about the full gamut of transition and shared that wisdom with others going through transitions of their own. She offered herself to others coming out of the American Evan-gelical faith—tired, broken, and hurt by their loved ones. She offered hope to each of the weary and disaffected, one lunch date at a time.

A friend who identifies as a gay Christian found a new calling when she met Paula for the first time. "The most sig-nificant thing she said to me in our first conversation was, 'Embedded in your identity is a responsibility to be a voice for change.' That has always stuck with me. To me, it was like God speaking through her to me. And I think that 'calling,' so to speak, gave me courage to move forward."

My dad's coming out gave her life a new calling by which to live. Embedded in her identity was the same responsibility to be a voice of change, and for that I celebrate my dad's transition.

Queer-identifying friends at my church talked about meeting Paula at the conference of the Gay Christian Network (now Q Christian Fellowship). She made time to offer encouraging words and a challenge to each of them to continue to live their truth. I'm thankful that her authentic identity gives others the courage to shed their false selves and to do the same.

I felt safe with her friends.

Someone asked a more direct question: "Knowing all that you know, would you want your dad back the way you knew him, as a man?" And the answer is yes. Knowing all that I know now, there are times when I want my dad back as a man.

My buddies Adam and Greg told me about the trip they took with their dad to Alaska. They caught some salmon and had a few beers, and planned out the trip they'd take together the next year, just father and sons.

They talked about packaging fish and hiking through mountains, and conversation that comes with the fact that a group is bound by choosing and maintaining a male identity. I couldn't consider an experience like that of my friends. That experience was gone from me, and I privately lamented that fact like I do so many others.

I miss the camaraderie I had with my father. My father's transition brought with it unfamiliarity. I had to get to know her again, and our times together consisted of creating a functional framework with a brand-new person who never actually left. The intention of each visit, to consciously invite her into my life as Paula, continues to be emotionally exhausting, and sometimes I think back to the familiarity in which my dad and I lived, and I miss not having to carry the burden of intentionality.

For my sisters and me, my father's transition opened up a Pandora's box of our own shortcomings, exposing places once nestled deep in our subconscious. Having spent most of my life dealing with issues of anxiety and depression, my father's transition exacerbated both, which still have the potential to threaten my well-being. My wife spent a good deal of her grieving giving support to my grieving. With that comes resentment and conflict. My sisters dealt with similar pain and struggle, which led to the unraveling of some of their deepest relationships. For those reasons, I prefer that my father's transition had not taken place.

My parents were married for forty years before my father decided to transition. My father's transition brought with it the uncoupling of my parents. There is a deep love and bond between my parents, and yet they are no longer together. My parents are incredible friends, but they no longer share the simple intimacy of being husband and wife. Navigating the new reality of my parents' relationship brings its own mourning for my family. The continued uncertainty of what it means for my parents to remain intentionally uncoupled adds its own unintended emotional weight.

At our worst, it feels like our family system has the potential to collapse at any moment, with any one of us becoming estranged and distant. My father acted as a linchpin, and it was pulled. My family struggles to build a new framework for our life with our dad living as a woman.

"Yeah, I think there are times when I wish that things would go back to the way they once were," I told my dad's friend.

"What's the hardest part?"

The conference was about to start, and I gave some consideration to politely ending our conversation, but instead, I pressed on, trying to articulate that which was the most difficult to say. How do I explain what I'd lost?

I'm a pastor because it's what we do in our family. I'm a pastor because my father was a pastor. When it was time for me to think about starting a new career and getting a new job, I knew that pastoring was the most distinct of possibilities. Jubi had worried that our move into ministry was not so much for me as it was a way to express devotion to the only person who could give me true validation. Who was I? I was Paul's son.

In the early days of my ministry, I was often introduced as such: "This is Paul's son. He's on staff at a church up in New York."

As a child, the words "This is Paul's son" were often met with a chance to hold my head high and bask in the glow of a proud father.

The same was true as an adult: "This is Paul's son. He's in ministry up in New York." My age was inconsequential. Being an adult with my own children mattered very little. I stood tall, knowing that being Paul's son in the ministry brought joy to Paul. I was Paul's child.

When I joined the ministry, it was my dad's theological leanings that largely drove my own thinking. Like-minded pastors who shared a similar theological framework became fast friends as we shared in a common ideology—my father's.

Each interaction I had in the realm of ministry was articulated with my father in mind. What would Dad think of this message? What story might fit him? I preached for twenty-six minutes instead of twenty-two minutes. My dad would have told me to cut out those minutes.

How would my dad handle the difficult elder? I know he'd ask them to leave. Do I have the same authority as my dad?

Every ask for money from the big churches, every idea shared with a pastor who had twice my experience, every workshop led, every impromptu discussion brought with it the thought that the interaction should be pleasing to my father.

In the most literal sense, it was my father who was my God. To whom do I belong? I belong to Paul, my father, and I believe that my work makes him well pleased.

I told my dad's friend, "In so many ways, the reason I'm even at this conference with you right now is because our church decided to be inclusive and affirming, in part, because of my father. That's what brought us here to meet you. One day, my father came to my home and told me that he wasn't really my father, and I lost the person who validated my whole ministry and my whole being. And that's the hardest part of my dad's transition."

My dad's new friend gave me a long hug that was wholly appropriate, regardless of the fact that our friendship was only minutes old. We made promises to talk again throughout the week of the conference, and I found a seat. For a fleeting moment, I realized that this conference was the first time that very few knew that I was Paula's son. I thought about keeping it that way. I didn't have to let people know that we were connected in the most meaningful ways. I thought about the merits of the church I led and whether or not the work we'd done would be credible on its own.

To my new friend, let me say now that I'm glad that my father transitioned and lives out life authentically, fully, and happily. My dad's life is changed, and it's good. And yes, I do struggle with wanting my dad back, but that's not because I don't believe her to be authentic or whole. It's because I must now work to answer the question of who I truly am, and that's a burden that, at times, feels insurmountable. But that burden is good.

In the beginning when God created the heavens and the earth, the earth was a formless void and darkness covered the face of the deep, while a wind from God swept over the face of the waters. Then God said, "Let there be light"; and there was light. And *God saw that the light was good*; and God separated the light from the darkness. God called the light Day, and the darkness he called Night. . . .

Then God said, "Let the earth put forth vegetation: plants yielding seed, and fruit trees of every kind on earth that bear fruit with the seed in it." And it was so. The earth brought forth vegetation: plants yielding seed of every kind, and trees of every kind bearing fruit with the seed in it. *And God saw that it was good.* And there was evening, and there was morning, the third day. . . .

God made the two great lights—the greater light to rule the day and the lesser light to rule the night—and the stars. God set them in the dome of the sky to give light upon the earth, to rule over the day and over the night, and to separate the light from the darkness. *And God saw that it was good. . . .*

So God created the great sea monsters and every living creature that moves, of every kind, with which the waters swarm, and every winged bird of every kind. *And God saw that it was good.* God blessed them, saying, "Be fruitful and multiply and fill the waters in the seas, and let the birds multiply on the earth." (Gen. 1:1–4, 11–13, 16–18, 21–22)

Good has become an unimaginative word. It's used for any number of reasons. To say something is *good* often masks the greater feelings and observances lying below the surface. *Good* is our lazy attempt to classify deep-seated feeling and emotion. If the facets of life feel simply average, or in balance, we might qualify our stability by saying that things are *good*.

The Hebrew translation of this word, *good,* is *tov.* At friends' celebrations, I shout the words *"Mazel tov!"* wishing them good luck, and yet this is the word attributed to God in the midst of the enormous and unimaginable movement of creation. It's far bigger than a celebratory reminder. What does *tov* truly mean, and why is it attributed to God's creation?

In a 2016 podcast, author and speaker Rob Bell refers to the most articulate definition of *tov* as, "for its intended purpose."[1] When God gives breath to all creation, God is basically saying that all of this incomprehensible and infinite matter is for its intended purpose.

We have night and day. Our days are bright and full of life. Our days are filled with energy that needs to be expended through work and physical activity. Our days are given meaning through the numerous interactions we have as we navigate the energy and the nuances of life.

Then God created night, an isolating time when our bodies rest. Our nights come with little energy expended and fewer interactions. Night becomes the time when our bodies are restored so we can meet another day. God says that those juxtapositions are *tov*. They're good. They're for their intended purpose.

God creates seed-bearing plants that grow and produce more seed-bearing plants. I love this. In order for seed-bearing plants to grow and thrive, they have to die. They go back into the ground and create nutrients for the plants that come next. They must give up seeds in order for there to be new life. Plants innately sacrifice parts of themselves for new growth and life. For a seed to create new life, it has to be buried. For new plants to grow, there has to be death. God says this is *tov*. This is good.

God made the stars, which bring light because they're dying. They are flaming balls of gas that come from dying planets and bodies. God says it's *tov*. It's good.

God brings animals of all types. God creates humans. God brings them forth to be fruitful and multiply.

The birth of my first child was a moment of great gratitude, joy, and celebration, profound in its act. It was also painful, terrifying, and traumatizing to both mother and child. Frankly, my children's births were by far the messiest, most gut-wrenching, bloodiest thing I have ever witnessed.

When my children come to me with scrapes, bruises, and bumps, I remind them that I watched them leave the birth canal and enter this world. That is far worse and more dizzying than falling off of the monkey bars.

"You've been through worse. Go and play."

Once we're out in the world, we're in a drop-dead sprint toward death, our bodies' atoms living and dying along the way. Science tells us that our atoms live and die so quickly that we're basically made up of completely new atoms about once every seven years. That's right. We remain uniquely "us" while our atoms go about the rapid process of living and dying. It's all for its intended purpose.

The great joy, celebration, pain, and trauma of birth hold true for just about every living thing. When God says that creation is good, God is saying that it is created for its intended purpose. That means that *good* doesn't always mean life will be okay. In fact, when God says that something is *tov*, there is usually light, growth, and birth, followed by darkness, pain, and death. *Tov* means that the fullness of life often comes with pain. It means that we won't always have the answers we want. It means that our shouts of, "Why God?" will feel like they're falling upon deaf ears. But it's "good," which means that creation will work according to its intended purpose. Sometimes that purpose means devastating pain. But *tov* also means that pain will turn from darkness to light and from death to resurrection.

There are times when I feel immense guilt over the pain that came from my father's transition to the female gender. For my father to be free meant that I took on her story, but led a very different journey. For my father to be her true self, I went through the stages of grief. I spent a chunk of the past few years depressed over the loss of my identity. My anger expressed itself in doubts over my father's mental well-being. In my denial of myself, I denied my father. I decided estrangement was an easier path than affirming her struggle. I didn't want to know her name. I didn't want to see my father in her feminine and most comfortable form. She courageously wore her journey. I, in my denial, did all I could to minimize her courage and her very being. I felt guilty for wanting my father to return. I felt guilty because, if I could keep my father, then I could keep my identity.

—✐—

After my father's transition and break with the Harvest Network, my father called to let me know she wanted to give living as Paul another chance. The burden of her Evangelical Christian ethos was lifted with her dismissal, and it was possible that Paul needed only to be freed from those shackles and not the shackles of gender fluidity. She wanted one more chance to salvage the familiarity of her life as Paul. She wanted one more chance to provide stability for her family. For a short period of time she made a brief transition to living life once again in the male-identifying gender.

Our family had already scheduled a visit to my parents. My father and I decided to go mountain biking. It's cold in the high desert, especially in the middle of February, and our earnest attempt at biking was continually thwarted by the presence of ice. Every hundred yards or so, my father and I would have to dismount our bikes and walk a few feet over the ice before resuming the ride.

Once or twice I led the way and literally fell flat on my face from the black ice on the trail beneath. We laughed at my misfortune. We talked, laughed some more, and started riding up the winding east side of the mountain. The elevation gain was rapid, and the trail was only wide enough for one rider at a time. We couldn't ride side by side.

I came across a large patch of ice, dismounted my bike, and began the trek up the icy trail, only to lose my footing. I loosened my grip on my bike handlebars, and immediately my bike fell off of the side of the mountain about ten feet into the brush below. I nearly fell with it.

I shouted a warning to my father, who was a few yards behind me, and slowly lowered myself down the side of the trail to retrieve my bike. With great difficulty, I grabbed my bike and dragged it back through the brush, up the mountain, and onto the trail. It took a few minutes to get back up to the trail, including a few slips and falls.

When I finally made it back onto the trail, I saw my father. He was laid out on all fours; his bike fell off the trail and lay a few feet from where mine had recently been. My father tried to crawl along the icy trail, his biking cleats slipping with each movement.

My father steadied himself on the ice and tried to crawl again, but with no luck. His bike cleats slipped again, and he was within a couple of feet of sliding off of the trail and down into the brush below.

I began the perilous walk over to my dad from just a few feet away. I wasn't crawling, but I was well aware that with each step, I might go over the side myself.

"I can't do it! I can't do this! I can't make it." I recognized my father's anxiety. It was the same anxiety and frustration that surfaced in me as a child. It was the same anxiety and frustration at the distinct possibility that we'd miss our trip to Washington, D.C., or that I would have to attend summer school: "I can't do this."

I dropped to the ground and slid on the seat of my pants over to where my father clung. I helped position my father in such a way that he no longer was at risk of falling. I lowered myself ten feet down into the brush to retrieve my father's bike. I slowly made my way back up, my father clinging desperately to the trail above.

Slowly, with our bikes dragging behind us, we shimmied back down the steeply graded trail to a safer spot below. Neither of us spoke for a few minutes, still processing the stupidity of biking on ice. My father broke the silence.

"This is not something I can do, Jonathan."

We walked our bikes the rest of the way back to flat ground.

My father was truly born again. She made the courageous decision to be birthed again, with all of its drama and pain. She decided to take new breath in this world, with all of the hurt that goes with it. She decided that her journey was authentic and worth living, even if it meant that parts of it must die. I didn't want to stand in my father's way. Paul wasn't my father's journey to live anymore, and it was for its intended purpose.

In the moment of driving back down the icy roads from the trailhead, I knew that my father's transition to the female gender was good. It was inevitable that the next time I saw my dad, she would be Paula again. And if that was the case, then it was okay for me to be vulnerable. It was okay to be sad. It was okay to mourn my father. I was free to be angry. I was allowed to cry in the green room. I could tell my staff. I could let them comfort me. I didn't have to be a perfect leader. I realized that the pain I was feeling over my dad's transition was *tov*. It was for its intended purpose. My pain was good. It was righteous. It was bringing about resurrection and new birth.

Paula's transition freed me to find my own identity and to make my own way in the world. Creating my own identity would have its dark nights and regressions. Pursuing my own identity would bring about little deaths, and they could occur only with honest feelings of loss, brokenness, pain, and estrangement. I knew that fighting through those feelings would bring about new birth in me too.

My father's transition loosed me from her, and it was for its intended purpose. It was good.

The larger questions still remain: Do I have any business leading a church? Is this my calling or my father's? Do I believe in the good work our church is doing, or am I simply following in my father's passion and journey?

There's continual and honest assessment as to whether or not my true self wants to lead others down the path that my father trod and his father before him. Is it possible that I need to find a new line of work in order to find my own uniqueness? It's certainly a possibility. The bigger questions relating to my work still need time to die and be reborn. My father's transition was years in the making, and her metamorphosis continues. I expect mine to take time as well. In the meantime, I give special attention to the little deaths along the way. They hasten my path toward my rebirth.

Even the minutest decisions are deaths and rebirths. We bought a car recently, and decided on a brand different from the ones my father owned. While this might seem innocuous, and even trite, it speaks to the depths to which I identified as my father's child; I count each small step as a new, painful, traumatizing birth.

I love my dad dearly. She's an incredible woman and an incredible friend. She's allowed me to experience the grief and pain I need. She's been gracious with my misplaced anger. I affirm my father and am thankful for the newfound peace that she has found. I'm especially thankful that her transition has led to one of my own.

I still wish that my dad crossing his legs and clapping politely during a hockey fight might have clued me in sooner. Perhaps I would have been spared the pain of the deaths and births that make up my new identity. I'm fairly certain that developing a new sense of self in the middle of one's life is not optimal. The harder one falls, and the later in life, the longer it takes to heal. The scars don't go away. But maybe that's okay.

A few months ago, I stood up in front of our church leadership and let them know that I had no idea what I was doing: "I don't know how to lead. I've not led on my own before, as my entire construct of leadership needs tearing down. I'm going to ask each of you to give me grace as I lean into my strengths and allow my weaknesses to die. I ask that you hold me accountable if you don't see me doing the hard work of transforming my leadership."

I wasn't giving up my father. I was giving up who I thought I needed to be for my father. My father didn't need me to lead in his or her image. My father didn't need me to espouse her values or structure of leadership. Paul hadn't needed that either. What I now know is that my father's prayer was for me to be my true and authentic self, my own person, one who belonged to the infinitely loving Creator, with all the inherent flaws that come with it.

I told my leadership that there would be pain in my self-discovery, and I hoped that they would walk with me through it. The leadership of our church prayed with me and for me. They encouraged my search and allowed me to embrace pain, knowing that new life comes at every turn.

My pain is good. My father's transition is good. The vulnerability of our ministry is good. The uncertainty, anger, sadness, hope, and joy are all good. They're *tov*. They're for their intended purpose.

I got tickets in section 110 for fifty-two bucks each. We sat just to the right of the first-base line, about eight rows up from the field.

"I can't believe you got these so cheap!"

I don't know that I'll ever get used to my dad's new voice. I'm not sure I'll ever get used to the fact that, when I give my dad a hug, I invariably come into contact with her breasts. There's much about my father's transition that doesn't make sense, and I don't believe that it has to. What makes sense is to celebrate daily that my father gets to live the rest of her life freely.

I bought the tickets to the game and went out to Denver to meet my dad so that we could watch our beloved Mets together. She bought herself peanuts and a soda, and I remarked that some things never change. The Mets, in the midst of a slump, played a game worthy of their frustrating season. We simultaneously remarked that some things never change.

The woman sitting next to us turned to join our conversation. "Are you from here?" she asked. I still wonder if they know that they're talking to my dad. My father pointed to me and told the woman that I was her son, visiting from out of town. I told her that we used to go to Mets games growing up. We had season tickets from 1987 until 1995. She said that she was impressed that a son and his mother could share that kind of love for baseball. That didn't happen too often, especially thirty years ago, implying that the role was generally reserved for dads.

My father continued to chat with the woman. They both mountain biked. My father mentioned that she was in her sixties and still rode every day, and the woman gave her a high five and called her a "badass woman." They talked about bike tires and the best places to ride during cold weather. My father told her about crawling on her hands and knees on the icy trail and emphatically said she had "no interest in ever doing that again."

Their conversation ended, and the woman left to grab more refreshments. My father and I sat and watched the Mets' prized rookie shortstop take his at-bat.

I waited for the feeling, the sense of loss and whatever form of grief might follow. It's always triggered by the stark realization that my father isn't the person I knew any longer. That feeling didn't come. My father was free, and I was free with her. I was free to no longer be tethered to her being. I was free to enjoy my father and celebrate the fortitude and fearlessness of her journey. I celebrated the fact that she was indeed a "badass woman."

We sat silently and wholly comfortable in each other's presence. We talked about the game, an upcoming vacation for my father, and a freak snowstorm in the mountains in late August.

The Mets lost the game, and my father and I walked out of the ballpark together. I gave my father a hug and told her that I looked forward to seeing her again. For the first time in a long time, I meant it.

I went back to where my wife and sister were staying. With an almost resigned concern, my wife asked me about the game.

"It was really good," I told her.

"What did you and your dad talk about?"

I thought for a moment. "We talked about the Mets and mountain biking. We talked a little about church stuff. Mostly we just watched the game."

"And that was good?" she asked.

I watched as the tension she visibly carried left her body. She searched my face and smiled, knowing that what I told her was the hard-and-fast truth.

"Yeah. It was really, really good."

NOTES

CHAPTER 1: THE VISIT

1. C. S. Lewis, *The Lion, the Witch and the Wardrobe* (New York: Collier Books, 1950), 75–76.

2. Paul S. Williams, "What Kind of Church Is This," *Christian Standard* (July 2012): 6.

3. *DSM–5* is the fifth and most recent edition of the *Diagnostic and Statistical Manual of Mental Disorders*, published by the American Psychiatric Association.

4. "Definitions," Trans* Awareness Project, https://www.transawareness.org/definitions.html, accessed March 1, 2017.

5. Walter Bockting, "The Psychology of Transgender," American Psychological Association (November 19, 2015), http://www.apa.org/news/press/releases/2015/11/psychology-transgender.aspx.

6. Bockting, "The Psychology of Transgender."

7. "What Is the Difference between Trans*gender* and Trans*sexual?*" Trans* Awareness Project, http://www.transawareness.org/what-is-the-difference-between-transgender-and-transsexual.html, accessed March 1, 2017.

8. *Merriam Webster*, s.v. "transvestite," last updated February 18, 2018, https://www.merriam-webster.com/dictionary/transvestite.

9. Katherine J. Wu, "Between the (Gender) Lines: The Science of Transgender Identity," Science in the News (Harvard

University, October 25, 2016), http://sitn.hms.harvard.edu/flash /2016/gender-lines-science-transgender-identity.

10. Giuseppina Rametti et al., "White Matter Microstructure in Female-to-Male Transsexuals before Cross-Sex Hormonal Treatment: A Diffusion Tensor Imaging Study," *Journal of Psychiatric Research* 45, no. 2 (February 2011): 199–204.

CHAPTER 3: FAMILY BUSINESS

1. See Ken Wilbur, *A Brief History of Everything*, 2nd ed. (Boston: Shambhala, 2007), 288–90.

2. Mary Collins and Donald Collins, *At the Broken Places: A Mother and Trans Son Pick Up the Pieces* (Boston: Beacon Press, 2017), 8–9.

CHAPTER 4: CRYING IN THE BACK OF A CAB

1. "Church Clarity Scores Outreach Magazine's '100 Largest Churches in America,'" Church Clarity, https://www.church clarity.org/100.

CHAPTER 6: MEETING PAULA

1. Julie Bakker, University of Liege, Belgium, European Society of Endocrinology, 2018 Annual Symposium, May 22, 2018.

CHAPTER 7: AT THE BRIDGE

1. M. Arbeiter, "15 Facts about the Brooklyn Bridge You Won't Fuhgeddaboud," *Mentalfloss.com*, September 28, 2010, http://mentalfloss.com/article/69143/15-facts-about-brooklyn -bridge-you-wont-fuhgeddaboud.

CHAPTER 8: FROM THE MOUTHS OF BABES

1. PFLAG, "Our Trans Loved Ones" (2015), 22, https://www.pflag.org/sites/default/files/Our%20Trans%20Loved%20Ones.pdf, accessed March 1, 2017.
2. PFLAG, "Our Trans Loved Ones," 22.

CHAPTER 9: INCLUSION

1. Elizabeth Dias, "Inside the Evangelical Fight over Gay Marriage," *Time* (January 15, 2015), http://time.com/3668781/inside-the-evangelical-fight-over-gay-marriage.
2. John Leland, "Faith and Family in Transition," *The New York Times* (June 16, 2017), https://www.nytimes.com/2017/06/16/nyregion/forefront-pastors-father-became-a-woman.html.
3. Andy Hill, email message to author, February 21, 2018.

CHAPTER 10: A JUST AND GENEROUS CHURCH

1. Rabbi Jon-Jay Tilsen, "Cross Dressing and Deuteronomy 22:5," *Dvar Torah* (Congregation Beth El-Keser Israel), http://www.beki.org/crossdress.html, accessed March 1, 2018.
2. Colby Martin, *Unclobber: Rethinking Our Misuse of the Bible on Homosexuality* (Louisville, KY: Westminster John Knox Press, 2016); Matthew Vines, *God and the Gay Christian: The Biblical Case in Support of Same-Sex Relationships* (New York: Convergent Books, 2015).
3. Rob Bell, *What Is the Bible? How an Ancient Library of Poems, Letters, and Stories Can Transform the Way You Think and Feel about Everything* (San Francisco: Harper One Books, 2017).
4. Derek Flood, *Disarming Scripture: Cherry-Picking Liberals, Violence-Loving Conservatives, and Why We All Need to*

Learn to Read the Bible Like Jesus Did (San Francisco: Metanoia Books, 2014), 74.

5. D. Eng, email message to author, February 22, 2018.

6. D. Eng, email message to author, February 23, 2018.

7. Diana Butler Bass, "A Horizontal Church for a Horizontal Spirituality (N125)," nomad* podcast (July 8, 2016), http://www.nomadpodcast.co.uk/nomad-108-diana-butler-bass-a-horizontal-church-for-a-horizontal-spirituality.

8. Butler Bass, "A Horizontal Church."

9. Grace Dowd, email message and Google document to author, February 24, 2018.

10. Pierre Teilhard de Chardin, *Toward the Future* (Orlando, FL: Harcourt, Inc., 1975), 86–87.

CHAPTER 11: *TOV*

1. Rob Bell, "Episode 66 | Good vs. Perfect," *The RobCast* (January 17, 2016), https://robbell.podbean.com/e/episode-66-good-vs-perfect.

CPSIA information can be obtained
at www.ICGtesting.com
Printed in the USA
FFHW011825051118
49298794-53511FF

9 780664 264352